IT'S NO SIN TO BE SIXTY

A POSITIVE LOOK AT THE THIRD AGE

Neville Smith

A Redemptorist Publication

Copyright © Neville Smith, 2007

Published by **Redemptorist Publications**
A Registered Charity limited by guarantee.
Registered in England 3261721

First published October 2007
Second Printing February 2009

Front cover image: Shutterstock.com and courtesy of Neville Smith
Cover design: Chris Nutbeen

Layout: Rosemarie Pink

ISBN 978-0-85231-342-8

A catalogue record for this book is available from the British Library.

Printed by Graham & Heslip Limited Belfast BT6 9HF

Redemptorist
PUBLICATIONS
Alphonsus House Chawton Hampshire GU34 3HQ
Telephone 01420 88222   Fax 01420 88805
rp@rpbooks.co.uk   www.rpbooks.co.uk

*In thanksgiving for fifty years
in the ordained ministry*

Acknowledgements

I once heard Joan Bakewell, the writer and broadcaster, say that everyone has a book within them. This is now my second, and each has taken me about ten years to produce. The first was a book of prayers for people in hospital, a distillation of my years of experience as a hospital chaplain. This, my second, is a series of reflections on later life: what it means to find oneself growing older, if not actually old, and how that experience is related to our Christian faith and our understanding of the Bible.

The book would never have seen the light of day without the help of Penelope Mander, who, over a long period of time, has taken my inelegant typescript, and reproduced it in a format which met the specifications of the publishers. For their part, Marguerite Hutchinson, as commissioning editor, gently, but firmly and wisely, rejected my first effort, and provided me with the encouragement and creative brief to try again. Andrew Lyon, the copy editor, has seen the book through to publication. My wife, Anne, has shown great patience while I have disappeared for yet another couple of hours in order "to do some more writing". I hope the book justifies the help and support of so many people. I am grateful to them all.

Neville Smith
Trinity 2007

Introduction

The village of Castleton stands in the heart of the North Yorkshire moors. It forms part of the parish of which I was vicar more than forty years ago. Just off the main street is to be found "The Old Men's Park", an open space set on the brow of a hill and surrounded by a low stone wall. It is, in fact, the site of the original "tin church" of the late nineteenth century, and was replaced by the present building constructed of local stone, and dedicated as a war memorial, in 1926. The Old Men's Park fulfils the function of its name. It is a place where the older men of the village meet together and sit to reflect on the state of the world, the state of the village, the state of their lives and that of their friends, neighbours and relatives. Given the origin of their surroundings, perhaps they also reflect on the state of the Church. I find it a sobering thought that having been part of the village as a young incumbent, I am now old enough to be part of their company.

However, this rural scenario poses a number of questions. Who are the "old men"? How do we quantify or justify that description? At what point does a person become "old"? How do we define old age? Is there some chronological or physiological description? It is easy to be aware of these questions; all of them are related to the ageing process, or our personal experiences of the ageing process. Yet there are no hard and fast answers. When I was going about my parish-visiting in Castleton, from time to time I would call on Jack, a retired farmer who lived in a cottage on the main street. He was a widower, well into his eighties, but still active and able to look after himself with the support of his family. He would always ask me about "that poor old lady", who lived at the end of one of the yards just up the hill and behind the main street. "That poor old lady" was, in fact, several years younger than Jack, but crippled with arthritis, and virtually housebound.

That contrast is replicated many times over. It is impossible to say when our consciousness of later life breaks in upon us. There is no set date, no particular age, no significant birthday. Some of us move easily and unconsciously into later life. For others, there is a particular, defining moment – retirement, an accident, the onset of a debilitating or life-threatening illness, occurrences which remind us that we are not as young as we once were, and that we no longer have the physical, or perhaps even the mental and psychological, resilience of earlier years. Some of us seize the opportunities with which our later years provide us, to fulfil ambitions and aspirations which have had to be laid aside during the course of our working lives. And others among us deny, or try to deny, our arrival in later life, and carry on as we did when we were twenty or thirty years younger.

Whether we handle our arrival in later life well or badly, positively or negatively, with acceptance or denial, we shall probably all have one thing in common: we shall do a lot of remembering, reminiscing and reflecting. It is only natural that we should; we have far more of our lives behind us than before us. We have gained a lot of experience on our passage through life and our memories are an important part of us. The painful ones we cannot, nor should we, seek to deny. The enjoyable and happy ones we can go over, relive and take pleasure in again. It is perhaps by reflecting on the contrast between the two, the good and the bad, that we reach some kind of balance and a degree of calm, as we look back over our lives. In this book, I suggest that we use the same sort of process when we look at our relationship with God. We reflect on the way we have come, where we are now in our later years, on the way that lies ahead, and whatever it may hold in store for us. Just as many people use later life to explore new opportunities, so I suggest it provides us with the opportunity to reflect on our faith, explore new directions and themes within it, so that we deepen our understanding of, and enrich our relationship with, God.

Even though this is the aim of this book, I also suggest that our reflection on where God fits into later life can begin from many different points and various situations in life as we know it – sharing a drink with some friends in a pub, leafing through the newspapers and magazines just inside the supermarket, digging sandcastles on the beach, and having a disagreement with a neighbour over the garden fence. When I started to write this book, I was struck by how few references there are to older people in the New Testament; very different from the patriarchal society reflected in the Old. I wondered how I would manage to relate the themes and concerns of later life to anything I might find in the Bible. As I wrote, however, I realised how many of the incidents which I used as my starting points were reflected in incidents in the Bible, especially the Gospels, and these have become the focal points of the sections I have written.

In the process of writing, I have reflected personally, and find that the process has affirmed my perception of God, and, I believe, deepened my understanding of God. I offer it to you with the hope and the prayer that it will enable you to find that you, too, reach a new understanding of God, and are affirmed by what you learn and discover.

Contents

Things ain't what they used to be 11
The same – only different 14
Nostalgia...17
National remembrance......................... 20
Time...22
Remembering them as they were...............25
A young man's Gospel................... 29

Sacred space................................ 33
Going to church 37
Prayer: face to face with God.....................40
Crisis of faith...44
Faith 48
Religion and spirituality 51

It's okay to be me 55
Forgiving ourselves 58
Senior moments 61
What's in a name? 64
Self-esteem 68
The body 71
Dissonance in life 74
Life is an enigma......................................77

Half-empty, or half-full? 80
Digging the garden 83
Ageing is not for softies...............................85
Personal space 89
An attitude problem 92
Postcode lottery 95
Happy accidents 98
Defining moments 101
Stereotypes 104
Gentleness 107
A sense of humour 110
Decisions, decisions!................................114

Contents *continued*

The child within 118

A new member of the family...121

New freedom 125

In the middle of the night 128

Night is as bright as the day 131

Friends 135

Independence 138

Emotional fly-tipping..141

Touch 145

Christmas presents 148

Aloneness 151

Bad news 154

Our own mortality 158

D**** (the word we avoid) 161

Unfinished business 164

Vulnerability 167

Strain and stress 170

Pushing back the boundaries 174

Clearing out the clutter 177

Moving on 181

Travelling light 184

Use it or lose it 187

I am still learning 190

What a wonderful world...193

Things ain't what they used to be

I received a letter from my bank informing me that, as an improvement to the service they were offering their customers, all calls to my local branch would now be dealt with by a central call centre. I did not share the enthusiastic tone of the letter. Previously when I had telephoned my bank, my enquiries had been dealt with by Rebecca or David, promptly, personally, and extremely efficiently. Although I had never met them, and they were only voices over the phone, I felt that I knew them and could rely upon them. In return, they always seemed to recognise me. Now that has all changed, just as so much else has changed.

Those of us now in later life have been subject to massive change during our lifetime. Inevitably, the tide of change has swept through the Church. All denominations have been affected by the shift in outlook and attitudes of the last sixty years, and this has been reflected in their organisation, structure and liturgy.

In 1847, the Revd Henry Francis Lyte was about to leave the parish of Brixham, in Devon, where he had been incumbent for twenty-five years. Aged 54, he was suffering from tuberculosis, and, on the advice of his doctors, was moving to the gentler climate of the south of France. He took from his desk a poem which he had written some years previously for a dying friend. Now he too was dying. We know and use his poem, set to music, as the hymn "Abide with me". One of the lines which may strike us, and to which we may readily respond, is "change and decay in all around I see". There are times when we feel overwhelmed by change. Society, attitudes, outlooks, morals, acceptable behaviour, life itself – all is so different now from what we have known, grown up with, remember and still cherish. All too often, change seems to be the equivalent of, and to imply, decay.

It is easy for those of us in later life to talk like this, and in a sense it is natural that we should do so. Change can pose a threat to our way of life and our very being, just at that time of life when we are least adaptable, least able to cope with it, and at our most vulnerable. Yet if we can just manage to hold that first reaction, and move beyond it, we may be able to acknowledge that, in fact, change is the essence of life, and not only from a scientific point of view. We see change at work as we read the pages of the Bible. The Old Testament records the development of God's relationship with God's chosen people. When they failed to see or to be aware of this process, they were fiercely denounced by the prophets for being "stiff-necked". The religious leaders of Jesus' time were apparently no less so. He challenged them not only on the outward, ritual observance of the Jewish law, but on the inner meaning and spirit of the law: "The sabbath was made for humankind, and not humankind for the Sabbath." The most serious confrontation was when Jesus violently ejected the market traders and money-changers from the precincts of the Temple in Jerusalem: "Take these things out of here! Stop making my Father's house a market-place!" The implications which those words carried were enormous, and the claims could not have been more far-reaching. The ordinary people who heard Jesus preaching were aware that there was something special about him: "The crowds were astounded at his teaching, for he taught them as one having authority, and not as their scribes." Faced with such subversion, the Jewish authorities would only envisage one end. They could not accept the changes that Jesus demanded in the practice of their religion and in the way that their whole lives were constructed and regulated. In human terms, their will would prevail.

As Christians, we are therefore confronted with something of a paradox. Many of us in later life do not like or take very willingly to change. I certainly do not. Yet familiarity has perhaps blunted our perception of how much Jesus was an agent of change, and the fact that our whole Christian faith is really to do with change. On a personal level, our lives are changed, deepened and enriched through our encounter with the risen Christ. On a social level, in spite of its many failings, the Church has been active in bringing about change in many areas of life, improving facilities for health and education, and living standards generally, in many parts of the world.

So, in later life, we have to face up to this dilemma. Much as we may dislike change, and do our best to avoid it, realistically we know that we are caught up in the inevitable changes of the world around us, and that, as Christians, we are rooted and grounded in a faith, the essence of which is to bring about change. This means that, even at this stage of life, we need to ask ourselves what there is within us that needs to be changed, how we can bring about that change, and what the outcome might be. Perhaps the first change for all of us is to recognise that the only certainty in life is change itself. We can cope with that because we believe in the changelessness of God. An old prayer from the late-night service of Compline, an ancient service of reflection before rest at the end of the day, comes to my mind:

"Be present, O merciful God,
and protect us through the silent hours of this night,
so that we who are wearied by the changes and chances
of this fleeting world,
may repose upon thy eternal changelessness."

"O thou who changest not," wrote Henry Francis Lyte,
"abide with me."

The same – only different

Monet was famous for his paintings of water lilies in the garden of his house at Giverny. In his later years, he painted them many times over. The paintings were substantially the same, yet differing slightly in details of light and colour and the angle from which he painted them. As well as waterlilies, Monet produced a series of paintings of hayricks in a field in the countryside nearby, and another series of the great west front of Rouen Cathedral. He caught the stonework with the sunlight playing on it at various times during the course of the day. Again, the subject was substantially the same, but each finished painting was different from the others.

Caravaggio, in the seventeenth century, was another artist who painted the same subject twice. In this case, the scene was the Supper at Emmaus. In the earlier painting, the colours are bright, there is movement in the hands of those at table, and there is plenty of food on the table for them to eat. In the second painting, the colours are subdued to the point of being sombre, and there is little animation shown by those who share the meal. Even the hand of Christ, raised in blessing, hovers no more than a few inches above the table. The food is sparse, no one seems interested in eating, and sadness is etched on the faces of those who wait at table. By the time he painted the second picture, Caravaggio was a hunted man, on the run from the authorities after committing murder. Both he and the characters in his painting were the same, only different.

This same paradox was true of Jesus after his resurrection. He appeared first to Mary Magdalene. She recognised him, and talked with him. It was only when she touched him and tried to hold on to him, that he pushed her away: "Do not hold on to me." The risen Jesus was essentially the same, but at the same time different from the pre-crucifixion Jesus. It is no surprise, then, that he suddenly "came and stood among them", and, in contrast to his encounter with Mary Magdalene, "showed them his hands and his side". It was Jesus' command – to make physical contact with the wounds still visible on his risen body – that convinced Thomas that the resurrection was genuine. He walked with some disciples on the road to Emmaus, and broke bread with them in the inn at the close of the day. "Then their eyes were opened, and they recognised him; and he vanished from their sight." Jesus was essentially the same as he had always been, but because of the resurrection, he was now different.

As Christians, we are called to bear witness to the same paradox in our lives. "If you have been raised with Christ," writes St. Paul, "seek the things that are above." This is a high aspiration and we find it hard to live up to. Jesus sets the standard even higher. He says of those who follow him, "they do not belong to the world, just as I do not belong to the world." Yet all too often we do. We can find it difficult to straddle two worlds that are often in conflict: the vision of God's world set before us by Jesus, and the one in which we live. Even St Paul experienced the difficulty, and speaks for us all in his letter to the Church at Rome: "I do not understand my own actions. For I do not do what I want, but I do the very thing I hate." Perhaps so much later in time, and with so much psychological insight at our disposal, we do understand our own actions, and can acknowledge how they lead us into the internal conflict which Paul describes so succinctly. We know we should be different. At our best, we want to be different, and actively seek to be different through our commitment as Christian people. But we end up being depressingly the same, and not different enough.

Later life bears the characteristic of being the same, only different. Over the years, our bodies have been renewed many times over. Cells have died, and been replaced by new ones, but the new ones have not been quite the same, and we have undergone the process of ageing, gradually, and for the most part, imperceptibly. My hair is grey but I am unaware of when this happened, and how it happened. I am only conscious that it has. I feel no separation from the young man who looks out at me from the photographs of fifty years ago. I know it is me, and in some instances I can remember the photo being taken, and what I was feeling at the time. I am the same – only different.

The same is true of our religious faith and outlook. Essentially, our faith is the same, Christ dwelling in our hearts through faith, as we are, in the words of the letter to the Ephesians "rooted and grounded in love". But what may have started as a thankful acceptance of those words from the letter to the Ephesians, may now be subject to all kinds of questioning as a very necessary part of our faith in our later years. How does the faith of our youth relate to faith as we perceive and hold it now? We are the same – only different. But this paradox need not, and should not, overwhelm us. The scene of life moves on, the questions present and re-present themselves in many different ways, yet they are held within a constant framework: "Jesus Christ is the same yesterday and today and for ever."

Heavenly Father,
in whom we live and move and have our being;
you have been with us
all through our lives,
and have known at every stage of our way
how we have changed and become different,
yet remain essentially the same.
Be with us now in our later years,
and support us in the paradox of life,
that we may grow into the likeness of your Son,
Jesus Christ, who is the same
yesterday and today and for ever. Amen.

Nostalgia

Pardon the pun, but a video about the old Great Central Railway, on which I travelled frequently in my younger days, sets me off on a train of nostalgia. So do other things. When I see newsreel clips from the thirties when I was born, films from the forties when I was growing up, hear the music of the big bands of the fifties when I was a student, then a national serviceman, I enter another world. It is a world which is lost and gone for ever, yet a world to which I intrinsically belong, and where I feel at home. Its passing carries with it many regrets and a deep sense of loss, a sadness that the world of my childhood and youth is gone. It was a world where life was lived more slowly and graciously, it seemed, and trustingly too, so there is a very real part of me that regards it as precious, and wants to preserve it in some kind of way. Being realistic, I recognise that this is impossible.

It is like entering a room in the house where one has stored all kinds of souvenirs from the past. The room contains many memories – some happy, some sad. It brings to life again many thoughts and ideas, often long forgotten. It reminds us of people we have met and known at various stages of our life. Some we have lost touch with. Some will have died. But it is good to think of them again, and remember what we shared at the time. Having spent some time in this room, we must come away and shut the door firmly behind us, at least for the time being. We are aware that this is not a living room, a room in which daily life is conducted in its many forms. It is good to know that the nostalgia room is there, to visit now and again, but it is no substitute for daily life, and for real living.

Nevertheless, there is always the temptation to pass too much of our time in the nostalgia room, and there are occasions when we are encouraged to do so. Nostalgia has become big business. Many of the old 78 records have been remastered onto CDs. Coalmines, factories, cotton mills, canals, steam railways, dockyards have all been preserved, so that the rising generation might have at least some idea of how people used to live. A whole way of life has been reconstructed and preserved at Beamish in County Durham, while at Worksop in Nottinghamshire, Mr Straw's house, in the care of the National Trust, is like entering a time-warp. Nothing has been moved or altered since the family first moved in, in the 1920s. When we revisit the past in this sort of way, it can sometimes seem preferable to withdraw from the demands of life around us into a cocoon of nostalgia. It represents safety and security. The danger is that it may come to represent reality, and the life of the here and now an unwelcome intrusion. It is something which can happen little by little to any of us in our third age. It is, perhaps, the next step down the road after bemoaning too long, and too often, that things aren't what they used to be. Of course they are not. They never were.

I am reminded of the colourful phrase used in the Old Testament to describe people who were too set in their ways, and were unwilling to recognise the presence of God in their lives. "You are a stiff-necked people," declared Moses to the people of Israel. It is a phrase that is readily applicable to those of us in later life. We know all about stiffness and joints that are reluctant to move as we would want them to. So it requires little imagination to understand that stiffness can easily attach itself to our outlook on life in general, and our faith in particular. The past can be much more attractive than the present, or that even more unknown quantity, the future. It is easy to look back to a mythical golden age, when the churches were full, and the Christian faith had a firm hold over the hearts and minds of all believers. If this idyll ever existed, it was in a dim and distant past. Already by the mid-nineteenth century, the Victorian Church was battling with the problems of ministering to and seeking to convert the "labouring classes", as they were called. The Church into which I was ordained in 1957 was struggling with the problem of how to communicate the Gospel in the post-war world. The publication of *Honest to God* in 1963 came in many ways as a liberating influence, but now, more than forty years on, it is disconcerting to recognise that the questions posed by Bishop John Robinson have still to find a satisfactory answer.

Our faith does not allow us to be "stiff-necked". We have to look forwards and outwards, not only in our religion, but to embrace life itself. Nostalgia is part of us, an undemanding part, and a comforting part. But nostalgia is no way to live life, nor is it a substitute for life. Joyce Grenfell, beloved by many, and still fondly remembered, expressed this so well in one of her songs, written some ten years before she died in 1979:

> I wouldn't go back to the world I knew....
> It was narrow, small, tame, it had to go
> The world I knew, but it was fun then,
>   just the same.

"Amen" to that.

> *God our Father,*
> *creator of time,*
> *and giver of life,*
> *we give thanks*
> *for all that we have known*
> *and experienced in our lives,*
> *for people and places,*
> *for events and memories.*
> *Grant that all that has been,*
> *and makes us what we are,*
> *may enable us to embrace*
> *every aspect of life in the present,*
> *and bring us to be one with you*
> *in the eternal life made known to us*
> *in your Son, Jesus Christ our Lord. Amen.*

National remembrance

As I have grown older, I have found myself increasingly moved by acts of national remembrance. The process began some twenty years ago when I was working in Westminster. In the early days of November, I would go along to Westminster Abbey and spend some time in the churchyard where the Field of Remembrance had been laid out. I was deeply touched by the sheer number of wooden crosses planted in the earth, each bearing a poppy, and the name of someone killed or missing in action. Perhaps most poignant were the small plots of ground designated for service units which had long since been disbanded, or amalgamated into bigger formations. Even after a long period of years, there were always just a few crosses to affirm that those who had lost their lives were still remembered.

More recently, I toured some of the battlefields on the Somme in northern France, and was overwhelmed by the sheer size and scale of the military cemeteries there. Thousands upon thousands of names are inscribed on Lutyens' memorial at Thiepval, and on the Menin Gate at Ypres, where the Last Post is still sounded at dusk each evening, and still draws a large crowd of onlookers. At that moment, onlookers seem to be transformed into pilgrims, such is the power of that simple ceremony.

In 2005, I attended a service which marked the sixtieth anniversary of the ending of the Second World War. I reflected that I had lived in London for twenty-one years, just about the same time that elapsed between the two world wars. I was just eight when the war started in September 1939. Some sixty years later, I was conscious of how quickly that time had passed, and what it must have been like for my parents to be involved in a second major conflict after just a few short years, especially my father, who was wounded on the Somme. The notes of Last Post and Reveille were sounded under the church tower and soared upwards. Laurence Binyon's words from his poem "For the Fallen" were sung to a choral setting: "They shall not grow old, as we that are left grow old..." The tears came unbidden and overflowed. There was no holding them, and I felt no shame. They were part of what we were there for, and what the service was all about. We were remembering, and remembering in order to look forward. At that moment, we were laying the past before God in order to serve God better in the future. We pledged ourselves to work for a better world, in which peace and justice, forgiveness and reconciliation, acceptance and inclusiveness, would be available to all people, regardless of creed, colour or social distinctions. This is part of what we pray for daily in the Lord's Prayer: "Thy kingdom come" – even if there are all too few signs of this becoming a tangible reality.

So the words of Laurence Binyon resonate across the years, perhaps even more poignantly with the passage of time. We remember with gratitude those who died in battle for their country, and whose lives were cut tragically short. Their sacrifice lays upon us the responsibility for building a better world. But part of that responsibility is to care for those who do grow old, those who are wearied by age, and those whom the years condemn. "At the going down of the sun and in the morning" we must remember them all.

> *Father, we remember before you those who died*
> *in the service of their country,*
> *and those still living in later life.*
> *We commit them all to your keeping,*
> *in Jesus' name. Amen.*

Time

When we went on holiday to Tunisia, the travel company provided us with notes about the country. There was information about the political system, what people did for a living, their local customs, religious beliefs, and how they regarded time: "Time is more elastic than in most western countries. A thirty minute delay is considered to be on time, and Westerners must accept that this is not an offence, but rather a fact of life in this culture." So, forewarned, we were philosophical when events failed to start at the advertised time, or when there were delays in transport arrangements.

As it happened, our visit coincided with the end of Ramadhan, the four weeks in the year when Muslims fast from sunrise to sunset. The precise dates for the beginning and end of Ramadhan are fixed by sightings of the moon. It was expected that Ramadhan would end on the Tuesday or Wednesday of our stay, but which of these precisely would not be known until eight o'clock on Monday evening. The people of Tunisia accept this arrangement as part of their religion and culture and way of life. Our Western lifestyle simply could not cope with such a lack of precision, and such a degree of uncertainty. We cannot imagine not knowing until 24 December whether Christmas Day was going to fall on the 25th or 26th. Easter is fixed by the lunar calendar, but the dates are known and published years ahead.

Many of us live by the clock, the calendar, the diary. Our universal complaint is that we do not have enough time. I am constantly struck by the number of people who appear to be under pressure because of the constraints of time. Looking back over my working years, I am sure I was one of their number. Later life brings relief from the pressures and constraints of time, yet I am conscious of how many times I consult my watch during the course of the day. Old habits die hard. Apart from attending to the necessary duties and routines of daily life, there are few pressures upon me, and such as there are, they are usually those which I undertake voluntarily. Many of us are free to choose how we will spend our time. But at this point an important consideration presents itself: what choices will we make, and how do we reach our decision? The answers we come up with are far-reaching. The time we have at our disposal grows less, and therefore more valuable, every day that passes. It is vital, therefore, not to waste it, but to make the most of however much time remains to us. We are being encouraged increasingly to recycle everything possible. We are at last beginning to understand that the resources of the world we live in are limited and finite. We cannot recycle our time. That, too, is limited and finite, a fact which should concentrate the mind wonderfully in later life.

The early Christians had similar concerns, though in a rather different context. They were expecting the second coming of Christ, his return in glory to establish his kingdom, at any moment. Time was short, and they needed to be ready: "Be careful then how you live ... making the most of the time." St Paul urges Christians at Colossae to conduct themselves "wisely towards outsiders, making the most of the time"; and as for fellow Christians, he enjoins the churches of Galatia that "while we have time let us do good unto all, especially unto them who are of the household of faith" (KJV).

That urgency has faded with the passage of time, but the words still carry meaning for those of us in later life: use the time at our disposal, make the most of it. The message is clear, and even though we are aware of the limitations that age places upon us, we can still set ourselves achievable goals, and, even more, we can enjoy a real life-enhancing sense of satisfaction when we know we have reached them. How much better that is than the apologetic

23

admission that we never quite managed "to get round to it". There is no better way of being remembered than that we were people who lived life to the full, and made the most of the time that God gave to us.

Father eternal,
who entered our world of time
in the person of your Son;
enable us, we pray, in later life,
to achieve those goals
that are still available to us,
and be content in knowing
that we have used to the full
the time and opportunities
that you set before us,
in your Son, Jesus Christ, our Lord. Amen.

Remembering them
as they were

We remember our loved ones in a variety of ways. We may visit their graves from time to time, or go to see their names inscribed in a book of remembrance. Perhaps we put flowers in church, or ask that they be remembered in the prayers on the anniversary of their death. All these things are good to do. They make us feel close to our loved ones, bring us a sense of healing, and remind us, in our third age, that we hope to have someone to remember us when our time comes.

But I also like to think in less formal ways of those who have died. I find that if I recall their personal quirks in the ordinariness of everyday life, I remember them more frequently, and, for me, at least, they remain part of the family. My father, for instance, disliked washing up, and positively refused to wash the toast rack more than once a day. So I remember him daily as I stand at the kitchen sink after breakfast, or later, too, if we happen to have used the toastrack a second time. My mother was of an ultra-cautious disposition, always anticipating and preparing for a worst-case scenario, no matter how remote it might have been. So when I find myself exercising the same caution – "just in case", as she would say – I recall the enormous influence she has had on my life. I remember her younger sister, my aunt, when I am washing in the morning. Not long before she died, aged over ninety, I was having trouble with wax in my ears. "You should never wash them with soap," she said, quite sternly. The years rolled away, and there she was, addressing her young nephew, who really should have known better. The years roll away too, when I am encouraging our grandchildren to remember their manners. "He's a nice little boy," my grandmother would say of me, "but he sometimes forgets his yes-pleases and no-thank-yous." She was a pillar of the Church and my ordination was an answer to her prayers. I remember her with great affection.

These are all light-hearted moments, and each family will have its own way of remembering its departed members. But in their ordinariness, the moments carry something of the sacramental with them. They have a deeper meaning which enables us to remember, and even feel close to those whom we have loved and who now have died. It is almost as if they live again through those simple acts, through those quirky moments. Their memory is preserved by remembering them as they were, and not just in an idealised kind of way. "Everyone in their own life is a little bizarre, if not actually potty," wrote Jack Rosenthal, the TV dramatist. We remember our loved ones as they were, quirks and all.

The memory of the saints in the Church's calendar has become sanitised by the passage of time, and too many stained glass windows. We have come to invest them with a kind of passive holiness which, I am sure, is well wide of the mark. Take Willibrord, for instance, not a well-known saint, but one whose tomb I happen to have visited. He was born in the seventh century, studied under Wilfrid of York, became a monk in Ireland, then took the ultimate vow of poverty, leaving his monastery, never to return, being guided on his travels by God alone. His journey took him as a missionary to what is now Germany. He eventually became Bishop of Echternach on the border of Luxembourg and Germany, where he built a cathedral, and is now entombed. It was a long and arduous path that led him there, and he must have been a tough – and perhaps bizarre – character to undertake it.

Thomas More was canonised by the Roman Catholic Church for his martyrdom under Henry VIII, but Peter Ackroyd in his biography makes it quite clear that More was a man of his own time. He wore a hair shirt to remind him of the temptations and pitfalls that surrounded him. Archbishop Michael Ramsey is still remembered for his deep spirituality, but he was not an easy person to be in company with. He had no "small-talk" with which to ease social encounters, and with his height, hunched shoulders and shaggy eyebrows, he could be intimidating to young clergy such as myself. Yet we came to know that these traits were a cover for his painful shyness, especially when Joan, his wife, was not at hand. Once we understood this, we could appreciate his teaching and insight, and know that we were valued by a real father-in-God. Perhaps, in a way, his students and junior clergy were some compensation for the family he never had.

Donald Soper, or Lord Soper as he became, was a great advocate for the Christian faith. He was willing to pit his oratory and robust belief against all-comers at Speakers' Corner in Hyde Park for a great number of years, and well into his advanced old age. He was a fine example of a Christian who was willing to use all the quirks of his personality to the glory of God, and the greater understanding of those whom he encountered week by week.

This seems to be a quality which is lacking in today's Church, across the denominations, and in society as a whole. The refreshing, aggravating, inspiring and maddening "pottiness" that we need and even look for in our leaders is being replaced by a bland sameness and uniformity. No one wants to see a return to the cult of the individual. Too many dictatorships have marked the bloody history of the last hundred years. Yet we are not all the same, nor should we aspire to be. God has given us a host of different gifts, talents, insights, energies. All can be used in God's service.

At this time of my life, I read increasingly frequently the obituaries of my friends or contemporaries. I attend their funerals or memorial services. It makes me wonder in what way people might remember me. I hope it will be for myself, and who I was, rather than what I was, or whatever it was I managed to achieve. And if I am remembered for myself, I hope it will be for all the various parts that went to make up my personality, "a little bizarre, if not actually potty". In teaching his disciples, Jesus commented, "You will know them by their fruits." The fruits that we achieve in life bear the quirks of all that we are.

Loving Father,
you created us all to share
in the rich diversity of your gifts.
We give you thanks
for all those who have used those gifts
to serve you in many different ways,
and whose characters have been moulded
by your presence in their lives.
Accept us, we pray,
as we seek to bring
every aspect of our being
to the service of your kingdom,
and at the last,
gather us all
to be one with you,
in the name of Jesus Christ, our Lord. Amen.

A young man's Gospel

In his poem, "Evening Mass", Alex Smith, a good friend of mine of long standing, describes how "...The red lamps/of the choir stalls glow among the carved wood:/comforting Anglican aesthetics shroud/the oncoming night."

It is a scene which affects him profoundly, and reminds him of the passage of time and his own mortality: "I stand all too-knowingly in the flesh,/the gathered years disconsolate...". Then comes the phrase which has haunted me ever since I first read it:

"Christ was never middle-aged."

It is a statement so simple and obvious that I could not understand why it had never occurred to me before. Perhaps familiarity had blunted my perception of Jesus, even though I knew perfectly well that he was a man of his own time, and of his own Jewish background. Perhaps it was only in my own third age that I could begin fully to appreciate the implications of Jesus being the age he was. Others had got there before me. As I discussed my moment of revelation with Alex Smith, he told me that when Isaac Watts' great hymn "When I survey the wondrous cross" was first published in *Hymns and Spiritual Songs* in 1707, the second line originally ran "Where the young Prince of Glory died". The young Prince of Glory presents us with a young man's Gospel.

We can characterise the young man's Gospel which Jesus proclaimed with three powerful adjectives. The first is *urgent*. "Repent, for the kingdom of heaven is at hand" was Jesus' first message recorded in the Gospels. It underlay all his subsequent preaching and teaching. He presented people with a choice which they had to make there and then. "Follow me, and let the dead bury their own dead." For those who obeyed his call to follow him there was no turning back. "No one who puts a hand to the plough and looks back is fit for the kingdom of God." The second adjective is *uncompromising*. The parable of the Good Samaritan tells us to offer care and support to our neighbour, whoever and wherever they may be. But it also condemns those, like the priest and the Levite, who compromise their principles in reaching the decision as to what course of action they should take. So when Peter takes Jesus aside and suggests that he should make a compromise in order to avoid the suffering and ordeal which he has predicted lies ahead, Jesus rounds on him and condemns him: "Get behind me Satan! You are a stumbling block for me; for you are setting your mind not on divine things but on human things." There can be no compromise between the two.

The third adjective which characterises Jesus' message is *unrelenting*. Even at the moment of revelation of his true glory on the mount of transfiguration, Jesus is concerned with "his departure which he was about to accomplish at Jerusalem". For Jesus, that was the crucial moment in every sense of that word. From that time "he set his face to go to Jerusalem". Even when the disciples "entered a village of the Samaritans to make ready for him ... they did not receive him because his face was set towards Jerusalem"; there was no turning back. And Jesus made the same message clear to those who would follow him: "If any want to become my followers, let them deny themselves and take up their cross and follow me." He adds: "For those who want to save their life will lose it, and those who lose their life for my sake will find it." Elsewhere Jesus says: "Enter through the narrow gate... for the gate is narrow and the road is hard that leads to life, and there are few who find it."

The message is clear and unrelenting, as well as urgent and uncompromising.

Urgent, uncompromising, unrelenting, are adjectives which belong to people in the prime of their life. However, those qualities do not readily characterise the third age and many of us would have difficulty in owning them and relating to them. With the passage of time, we find that our sense of urgency fades, as does our ability to pursue our aims, come what may. Many of us have had to learn to compromise with the demands of our faith. We have often had to make difficult choices in order to deal with conflicting – and equally legitimate – demands on our time. And we may have to make a further compromise, between what we would like to do, and what we feel able to do. The spirit is indeed willing, but sometimes the flesh lacks the necessary energy. So uncompromising, unrelenting, and urgent we are not. We are probably content to pass on the missionary spirit to the younger generation.

This means a major readjustment in our understanding of the Gospel, and our relation to it in later life. We have to refocus our thinking. We have to move away from thinking of ourselves as those who, in obedience to the call of Christ, take the initiative in his name. Instead, we need to centre on God. In reality, it has always been God taking the initiative. It is always God who is urgent, uncompromising, unrelenting. "Lord, you have searched me out and known me," says the psalmist. God takes the initiative to seek us, find us, forgive us, restore us, renew us in God's image. We are never too old for that. We can be confident, knowing we are in his hands. In later life, we can rest content with the essential message of the Gospel.

Almighty God,
giver of health and strength,
we acknowledge before you,
and to ourselves,
that with increasing years,
our spirit is still willing,
but our body less able.
Help us to understand
the unfailing message of your love.
Seek us out and renew us,
restore us in your image,
so that we may be confident
and content in your presence,
and serve you to the end,
in the name of Jesus Christ, our Lord. Amen.

Sacred space

It is a long time now since I was in Jerusalem, but I still have vivid memories of my visit to that beautiful but troubled city. One of the sights which stays in my mind is of the "Wailing Wall", so called because it is the place where orthodox Jews come to say their prayers, and lay their penitence and petitions before God, volubly and audibly. It is their sacred space, because the place is more properly known as the Western Wall, the only remaining part of the Temple in Jerusalem, the magnificent building which epitomised for the Jews the glory of God, and in which the glorious presence of God resided. "In the year that King Uzziah died," wrote the prophet Isaiah, describing his vision of the glory of God, "I saw the Lord sitting on a throne, high and lofty; and the hem of his robe filled the temple." In John's Gospel, we read of Jesus' indignation that the glory of the Temple had been defiled by the mercenary grubbiness of the stall-holders and money-changers, those who made a living in the Temple precincts by trading on the religious traditions and observances of the Jewish people. "Take these things out of here," cried Jesus in righteous indignation. "Stop making my Father's house a market place."

It has always been important to be able to locate God, to create a sacred space or place which God was believed to inhabit. Thus Jacob wanted to mark the place and preserve the space where he had slept, and been caught up in the vision of the angels of God going up and coming down a ladder that reached from earth up into heaven. "Jacob rose early in the morning, and he took the stone that he had put under his head, and set it up for a pillar and poured oil on top of it. 'How awesome is this place,' he said. 'This is none other than the house of God, and this is the gate of heaven.'" In the New Testament, we find the disciples wanting to preserve the glory

33

of the vision in which they had shared on the mount of Transfiguration. "Master, it is good for us to be here," said Peter to Jesus. "Let us make three dwellings, one for you, one for Moses and one for Elijah." Perhaps as well as wanting to prolong the moment, Peter was responding to promptings buried deep in the ancient nature religions of his own people. The Old Testament prophets often spoke out against the sins of those who had turned away from the worship of the one true God, to indulge in the seductive fertility rites of the tribes who surrounded them. "The sin of Judah is written with an iron pen," thundered Jeremiah, "while their children remember their altars and their sacred poles, beside every green tree, and on the high hills..." In spite of Jeremiah's words, the desire or the need to locate God, or the gods, in the natural world, and to make appropriate offerings and sacrifices, was widespread in ancient times. The practice still flourishes in our own day, even in Western society, as well as in more primitive tribes and communities.

The spread of Christianity has been, and still is, characterised by the building of churches. These range in size and scale, from vast and beautiful abbeys and cathedrals, to the plainest redbrick chapels and the "tin tabernacles" of the nineteenth century. (The latter could be ordered as a kit from the catalogue of large department stores and builders' merchants.) Every group of like-minded Christian people that banded itself together, it seemed, raised the money to erect a building in which to worship God in their own particular way. On one level, the building represented an outward and visible expression of the faith of those who had subscribed to its planning and construction, and now were committed to maintaining it as a beacon of their special emphasis or understanding of the Christian message. On another level, the building represented a place where God could be found and known. It was the place where his presence could be experienced, and the experience shared with the other members of the worshipping community. Their common faith received its practical expression in outreach directed towards local people, and in pastoral concern for every aspect of their well-being. The mission of the Church remains essentially the same as it ever was. It emanates from the creation and provision of sacred space where the presence of God can be located. "You, O Lord, are in the midst of us, and we are called by your name." The words of Jeremiah in the Old Testament sum up what was to become the driving force of Christianity.

We therefore recognise within ourselves a deep-seated need for sacred space, or for creating sacred space somewhere to be able to meet and know God, and to be aware of God's presence. Many of us will find this in the churches and places of worship we attend week by week. There we renew our awareness of God, and are strengthened in our belief in God's presence in our lives by sharing our experience within the Christian community, the fellowship of the Body of Christ. But we may also find God in places that have no religious connection at all: the silence of mountains, the stillness of moorland, the rolling waves beating on the seashore, may all speak to us of God. A great painting, a favourite piece of music, words of prose or poetry may so resonate within us that we are able to be aware of God's presence.

Sacred space is by no means always tangible, identifiable, something "out there". Perhaps more often it can be something we recognise as being "in here". There is sacred space within us; sacred in the real sense of the word, meaning set apart for God. Something, or somewhere, that we share with God alone. "Commune with your own heart...and be still," says the psalmist (KJV). Perhaps some of the places where we find God will have to do with events in our lives, which we now recall; people we have met, known, loved; occasions which have served as turning points in the direction we have taken. The sacred spaces within us may centre on our personal thanksgivings, our successes and failures, our feelings of pain, joy and sorrow. They will include the elements of the relationships which have formed, and still form, the fabric of our lives. All this we are able to share with God in our own, personal sacred space. "God knows the secrets of the heart," says the psalmist. We meet God there.

But those secrets also contain within them a warning. The sacred spaces within us are not there simply to be nurtured for ourselves, savoured and enjoyed. We cannot cling on to or contain God. We have seen that Peter made this mistake on the mount of Transfiguration, and so did Mary Magdalene in the garden, where she was the first witness of the risen Lord. "Do not hold on to me," Jesus told her. Our own sacred space exists, whatever we may think or feel, to take us forward, lead us onward to an ever-deepening understanding of God, the way we have been led, and the way God will lead us still. Whatever sacred space we have known and valued in this life, it can only be a glimpse of the sacred space that God has in store for us in the life to come.

Heavenly Father,
we thank you
for locating your presence among us
in the person of your Son.
Enable us to make space for him
within our lives,
and within ourselves,
where we can share with you
the deepest secrets of our hearts.
As we glimpse your glory
in the sacred spaces of our lives,
lead us to that space
where we may know that glory in all its fullness
in your nearer presence,
through the same Jesus Christ, our Lord. Amen.

Going to church

In his poem "Church Going" Philip Larkin implies that we go to church for a variety of reasons, from savouring the silence, to responding to our innermost needs or deep-seated compulsions. The "blent air" of the church gathers together all those reasons, and – as Christians we would want to add – offers them to God.

I know that is true of myself. I go at least partly from habit. The church building and church service is part of me, and I feel something essential would be missing if I did not go. I suppose after so many years, I am hooked! I also go out of a sense of duty. When I consider the number of hours in the week, and the range of activities I pursue, it seems to me a poor and unbalanced sort of relationship if I am unable or unwilling to set aside some time to acknowledge the presence of God in my life, indeed the gift of life itself. I go because there are times when I need, as they say, to lay something before the Lord.

Other times I go because I feel I have nothing to lay before the Lord, I have nothing to offer. I feel the need to receive whatever God can give me to allay the emptiness inside. And if all this seems somewhat negative and lacklustre, I hasten to add that I also go to church because I want to, because I enjoy it (usually!) and because I find it affirming and uplifting. In later life especially, we may find reassurance in the familiar forms of worship, in the literary cadences of the Bible, and in the traditional structure of the liturgy. We can find in them true refreshment of soul, in contrast to so much around us that is cheap, noisy, tawdry and apparently pointless.

So the last thing I am looking for when I go to church is disturbance. I don't mean the casual disturbance of a persistent cough or a noisy child, but deep, inner disturbance. Paradoxically, what causes me such disturbance is the very fact of being in church. On one hand, I am confronted with life as it could be and should be, the vision of "life in all its fullness"; and on the other, life as I experience it and know it to be. On one side of the divide, there is goodness and compassion, understanding, forgiveness and acceptance, embodied in the person of Jesus. On the other, there is unending violence and degradation of the human personality, and all the negative elements of life which need no spelling out. Somewhere in the middle of this great divide is me, torn apart inwardly by this disparity, trying to understand it, doing my best to make sense of it all, and somehow seeking to hold together all the conflicting elements in tension. They constitute a forceful reminder of the words of Jesus "My kingdom is not from this world", and of the inner conflict facing the disciples: "You do not belong to the world, but I have chosen you out of the world." The counterclaims of this dual loyalty still remain to be resolved by all who would seek to follow Jesus.

There still survives on the chancel arch of a few medieval parish churches a painting of the last judgement. Such paintings were common in medieval times and served as a solemn warning to people as to their actions and the quality of the lives they were leading. One day they would be called to appear before God, depicted in all his glory, and answer for all they had done or failed to do, according to Jesus' parable of the sheep and the goats. The sheep, those who were righteous, would be directed to enjoy the blessings of eternity at God's right hand. The goats, representing the wicked, would be banished to God's left hand, to undergo the flames of everlasting torment. It was all clear-cut and straightforward. There was no middle way. To the medieval mind, people fell directly into one category or another, and much time, energy and expense were directed towards trying to achieve heaven, rather than be cast into eternal hell-fire.

But we know that things are not as simple as that. Between the two extremes are many shades of grey, and I sometimes wonder whether the meaning of the parable of the sheep and the goats is as obvious as it appears to be. It struck me, when visiting Israel, that it can be very difficult at a glance to look at a mixed flock of sheep and goats and tell one from the other. Both sheep and goats look remarkably similar to the casual eye. So I ask myself whether there might possibly be a secondary, hidden meaning in the parable. Perhaps at the ends of the spectrum there are those who are patently good, and those who are notoriously bad. But probably most of us find ourselves somewhere in the middle. It is an uncomfortable position to occupy. Sometimes we veer towards one extreme, sometimes towards the other. We are a curious mixture of good and bad, aspiring to one, and succumbing to the other. Going to church reminds me that I am just as much a mixture as anyone else. We need to offer one another much patience, forbearance and forgiveness. Going to church, especially in my third age, reminds me of my continuing need for God.

Heavenly Father,
we give thanks for the opportunity
to worship you in church,
day by day, and week by week,
to offer you ourselves as we are,
to bring our needs,
and to offer you our prayers.
As we acknowledge the claims upon us,
made by your kingdom,
and the world in which we live,
strengthen us by your presence,
and fulfil our need for you
in every aspect of our lives. Amen.

Prayer: face to face with God

The first full week of July 2005 was, by any standards, a tumultuous one for London. It encompassed, within a few short days, the expression of the whole range of human emotions. It began with the Live 8 concerts, both in London and in some of the other most affluent cities of the world. Their aim was to express support for, and solidarity with, the world's poorest people, especially in Africa, and to "make poverty history" by exerting pressure on the leaders of the G8 nations meeting in Scotland the following Thursday.

On Wednesday came the news that London had succeeded in its bid to host the 2012 Olympic Games. However, the exhilaration was abruptly cut short by the suicide bombings on the London transport system the following morning, in which more than fifty people tragically lost their lives. On Friday, London was on the move again, with transport restored more or less to normal. On Saturday, the Queen unveiled a statue in Whitehall to acknowledge the enormous and varied contribution which women had made to "the war effort", from 1939 to 1945, and which had not been publicly or officially recognised previously. Finally. the week ended with services of thanksgiving to mark the sixtieth anniversary of the ending of the Second World War. For those of us in London, especially, it was something of a roller-coaster week which aroused a mixture of feelings and conflicting emotions.

I found many of them difficult to deal with. A friend of mine told me that she watched the TV reporting of the suicide bombings with tears rolling down her cheeks. Mine were not far behind. I was desperately sad for the families and friends of people who seemed simply to have disappeared. Yet I had to ask myself why I did not react in the same way when I heard on the morning's news bulletin that similar numbers of people had been killed by suicide bombings in Iraq, or that people had simply disappeared in Zimbabwe or other states with totalitarian regimes.

Similarly, I want to do all I can to make poverty history, but one does not need to be cynical or to have a lot of political insight to know how difficult it is to translate good intentions and beneficent decisions by the leaders of the richest nations into action that will relieve those people most in need. The problems remain as to how to bring them adequate food, sufficient clean water, the basics of health care, and primary – let alone secondary – education. It is a gigantic task which depends on so many interlocking factors.

Commemoration of the Second World War brings back disturbing memories. Even though I was only a boy at the time, I can remember enough and have read enough to know how deep the scars of war are. Victory was achieved only through enormous cost of human life and pain and suffering. It is that that we need to remember and bring before God, not in any triumphalist way, but rather in penitence for human selfishness, folly and weakness. It disturbs me enormously that in some ways, through the cinema and the media, we seem still to be fighting the war.

I find this conflict of feelings and emotions typical of what I try to bring to God in prayer. As I get older, I find that I am bombarded by images which pull me in all sorts of directions. So, for example, I start to pray for wisdom for the G8 leaders, but I slip into images of deprived people in Africa, who also need my prayers, as do the people caught up in the London suicide bombings, whose shocked faces are imprinted on my mind, as well as those who are traumatised by similar incidents in Iraq or other parts of the world.

What used to seem so simple now seems so much more complicated. I still have a book of prayers which I bought as a young curate, and used for intercessions at Morning and Evening Prayer for years afterwards. Tucked in the back are prayer cards produced by missionary societies and various good causes. The topics for prayer are brief and to the point. They were not hedged about with the constraints and limitations of which I am so conscious now. Prayer seemed easier and more direct. Life itself seemed less complicated. Perhaps I worry too much. I know that even though we may feel that our own prayers are inadequate, they are nevertheless gathered up into the constant prayer that the whole Church brings before God through its daily round of services and worship, especially in and through the Eucharist. As the old hymn puts it, "The voice of prayer is never silent, nor dies the strain of praise away."

Nevertheless, there are times when I feel that our services and liturgy sanitise our prayers, and, with the best of intentions, drain them of their urgency and immediacy. Perhaps the essence of prayer is that there is a confrontation with God. In prayer, we are meeting God face to face. There is energy, emotion, passion, as we find in the Genesis story, where Jacob wrestles all night with the angel of God. We find Jesus wrestling in prayer in the Garden of Gethsemane, bearing a conflict of emotions. He knows what lies ahead and shrinks from it: "Yet not my will, but yours, be done." On the cross, the horror appears to overwhelm him, and he cries out, "My God, why have you forsaken me?" Yet his last words speak of the certainty of achievement: "It is finished."

Confusion and conflict are not unknown to the risen Lord to whom we bring our prayers. They were part of his life from the moment he started out on his public ministry, and still are for us now who seek to follow him on the way. Yet there is no other way for us. He only has the words of eternal life.

Lord, when prayer seems feeble and beyond us,
help us to know that you, too,
lived with conflict and confusion,
and that all is gathered up into your eternal
offering to the Father,
in the unity of the Spirit,
one God for ever. Amen.

Crisis of faith

Each week, two free newspapers are pushed through our door. I usually skim over them to catch up on the local news, and to make sure that I am not missing out on anything of consequence taking place in our area. There are not many weeks that go by without a report that some older person has been the victim of a confidence trick. Usually, it is carried out with the utmost simplicity by trading on the trusting nature and general gullibility of many older people. Typically, a man with an official-looking uniform knocks on the door. He produces a bogus ID card, and tells the householder that he has come to attend to the gas, water, electricity – anything that will require his gaining admittance. He and his colleague are let in, in good faith, and while he engages the resident in conversation, his accomplice goes ostensibly to see what needs to be done to carry out the job in question. It is only when the pair have left, promising to come back later, that the old person realises that money or valuables have disappeared with them. Despite a spate of similar incidents and repeated warnings, older people still get conned.

I know the feeling. We were flying for a holiday outside the EU, so I bought some local currency at the airport before we left. The assistant suggested that I should pay a premium to make sure that I got back the full value of any currency that I had left over when I changed it back into sterling, in case the currency had dropped in value while we were away. As we were only going for a week, unless something catastrophic happened, that eventuality was not really likely to arise. But it was early morning, I find airports stressful, and I felt harassed. I was not hearing well, and did not really understand what the young assistant was saying. So I accepted his advice and paid the premium. Later, I was cross with myself because I knew I had allowed myself to be prevailed upon to pay for a financial protection which was unnecessary. The amount of currency I had bought was relatively small, and we were only going to be away for a short time. Fortunately, the extra premium was not large. It was the dynamics of what had happened that made me cross. I could not honestly say that I had been conned, but I knew that the situation had arisen because I am that much older, and no longer think as quickly as I once did.

Sometimes, I have to admit, I wonder whether the same thing is true of my religious faith. The doubts crowd in unbidden and sweep me along on their negative tide. I am, in later life, left wondering whether my faith is founded on nothing substantial, whether it is at best no more than wishful thinking and at worst a gigantic confidence trick. Paradoxically, these thoughts tend to arise when I am in church. I sit and look around me, most often in centuries-old buildings where it often seems, whatever the state of one's faith, that there is a special feeling, as if the walls themselves have been permeated by the worship of the faithful, and hallowed by the passage of time. Succeeding generations have devoted time, energy, expense and loving care to preserving such buildings to the glory of God and as an expression of their own Christian faith. I am aware of the service in which I am taking part, the words of the liturgy, the music of the organ and choir, the message of the scriptures, and the words of the preacher. I think of the vast institutional presence of the Church throughout the world, its power and its authority, the influence it wields, and the respect it commands. It is then that the shadow of doubt crosses my mind. I find it difficult to equate the Church as I know it, with all its wealth and power and possessions, with the humble, itinerant preacher who appeared briefly in Palestine some two thousand years ago, and who was quickly snuffed out by the religious authorities whose power and influence he challenged. The existence of Jesus is attested and verified by independent historical sources. Yet our whole faith is based on the claim that Jesus, having been crucified, rose from death. That is our baseline. Either we believe it, or we don't. It is essential to hold on to the belief, regardless of what the Church does or fails to be, regardless of what it preaches or fails to teach. Certainly something of major importance must have happened for a tiny sect, in a small part of the mighty Roman empire, to have become a worldwide religion. But whatever the evidence, no matter how compelling it may be objectively, each one of us has to make our own decision: is this a belief to which I can reasonably commit myself, or does it remain a man-made (and I use that adjective intentionally) confidence trick? Whichever decision we make, whichever side we come down on, we may find, naturally enough, that we wobble at times from one side to the other.

This can be especially important for us in later life, when we find that previous certainties in outlook, and accepted standards in common practice, are eroded, or even disappear altogether. It is easy to feel that the same thing is happening to our faith, which is in any case a grey area where, for many of us, uncertainties abound. I like to believe that God understands this, and accepts our moments of doubt, and the crisis of confidence which we suffer from time to time. One of my favourite encounters in the Gospels comes from St Mark, where Jesus affirms the scribe who is seeking to understand the fundamentals of his Jewish faith: "You are not far from the kingdom of God." Those words might affirm us all, as might those which begin Hebrews 11: "Faith is the assurance of things hoped for, the conviction of things not seen." For, writes St Paul, "what can be seen is temporary but what cannot be seen is eternal." Therein lie our hope for the Church (whatever form it may take) and our own personal faith.

Father,
we thank you
for the faith you have given us
in your Son, Jesus Christ.
Look graciously upon us
when faith falters
and doubt casts its shadow
over the brightness of our belief.
Grant us to know your presence
within our lives
and in the life of your Church,
that our conviction in things not seen
may carry us through the things that surround us
*   now in later life*
and into the life that is to come. Amen.

Faith

I write these words a few days after returning from a holiday in Italy. I have been there several times now. I love the warm sunshine, the colours, the food, the wine, the friendliness and welcome of the Italian people. And I am always attracted by the way they do things. Whether it is building bridges in impossible places, designing household goods for everyday use, or wearing fashionable clothes, Italians do it with style.

I am sure it is not difficult to understand the meaning, or appreciate the feeling, of what I am trying to convey. Yet "style" is difficult to quantify or define. One has only to think of Art Nouveau or Art Deco. Both are easy to recognise, but almost impossible to put into words. This is because style carries with it a mixture of the objective and subjective. Objectively, I see things in Italy: roads, bridges, household goods, clothes. Yet what I am describing, or trying to describe, is the effect they have upon me and my response to them.

I use this analogy because I believe it has something useful to tell us about the way we perceive our faith. Faith cannot be encapsulated. No definition can be put forward which can express all the myriad different perceptions of faith by which Christians practise their belief. The ancient creeds of the Church, which have been handed down to us, sought to codify Christian belief and set it on an agreed official footing. But the creeds themselves represent a compromise of what were held to be the essentials of the faith at the time, and were a mixture of historical fact, philosophical theory and poetic vision.

It can be difficult for us to feel that these traditional formularies, worked out so long ago, can be a satisfactory vehicle for the expression of our faith. We need to feel that it is vibrant and alive, not tied to the constricting demands of the past. Our faith bubbles up in response to all the new experiences of life in which we see the activity of God, and overflows, as it were, the official container. It is rather like fizzy lemonade or sparkling spring water being poured into a glass. We can see for ourselves just how much it froths and sparkles.

In our third age, we have the opportunity to review our faith. We look back at the way we have come. Perhaps there was a specific moment when we chose, actively and consciously, to commit ourselves to God. Or perhaps such a moment never occurred, because we were brought up in the faith, and it was always very much an essential part of us. Either way, it can remain difficult to define exactly what we believe, or why we believe it, or how strongly we believe it. I think I have always been aware of a tension deep within me, between official church teaching and my own personal faith. I have long been disturbed by the claims of the faith, and felt uncomfortable with the contradiction between the official expression of belief on the one hand, and on the other the world as I experience it and know it to be. Looking back, I think it was the recognition of this disparity which took me into the hospital ministry. Every day, I faced the division between the healing and redemption that the Church claims for the world through Jesus, and the pain and suffering of human affliction in all its various manifestations. In seeking to find some means of reconciling these two conflicting areas of human experience, I was not only ministering to others in their need. I was, I think unknowingly, ministering to myself in my own.

Yet like so many of us in our third age, despite all the contradictions and apparent evidence to the contrary, I have held on to, and continue to hold on to, my faith, though now I need to be more reflective, and leave more active ministry to those who are younger.

I still find it difficult, if not impossible, to define my faith. It would be so much easier if there were a series of multiple choice questions, preferably colour-coded, and all I had to do was to tick the right one. But faith, like style and love and beauty, defies definition. I love the opening verse of Hebrews chapter eleven: "Now, faith is the assurance of things hoped for, the conviction of things not seen." But for me, faith is even more basic than that. It is simply to make room for God in our lives – not as an insurance policy because time is running out, but because it is best for the here and now. What happens after is in God's hands.

Lord God,
the centre of all that we believe,
in our later years
give us the courage
to reconsider our faith,
to see it again
with fresh eyes and new interest,
to shake off old expectations,
and outworn ideas.
May our faith be renewed,
revitalised and reinvigorated,
so that it may sparkle again
with new light and new meaning
that will bring us close to you,
and deepen us and refresh us
in the love made known to us
in your Son, Jesus Christ our Lord. Amen.

Religion and spirituality

I have to confess that I came late to the realisation that religion and spirituality are two separate entities, and not one and the same thing. I trained for the ministry at a time when it was assumed that a person's religious devotion was the same as their understanding of the Christian faith and their spiritual depth. So, for instance, someone who attended church perhaps twice on Sundays, and one or more of the weekday services, was regarded as being devout and of spiritual depth. In the Roman Catholic Church, the Second Vatican Council called by Pope John XXIII in 1962 was pivotal in changing this attitude. In the following year, the publication by Bishop John Robinson of *Honest to God* was also of major importance, and blew fresh air into the corridors of the churches. They expressed for many of us something of which we were already aware: the gap which existed between the teaching of the Church, and everyday life as we knew and experienced it. And for this official recognition, we were grateful. It represented a release from false and unnecessary constraints, and unlocked a great deal of energy and enthusiasm among Christian people – laity and clergy alike.

Looking back, I suppose I was conscious of "ministering" religion, whereas what I really wanted to do was to exercise my ministry in such a way as to enable people to develop a spirituality which would help them to cope with, and make sense of, the situations they faced in their lives. This question was one which continually confronted me during my hospital ministry. It was intensely personal, and a constant challenge to my faith. Somehow, I had to be able to reconcile my belief in the self-giving, healing love of God, revealed to us in the dying and rising of Christ, with the pain and suffering on every level of human experience that was going on around me, and in which I was involved day by day. So often, I could see, what people wanted and needed was spirituality, to be able to make sense and to reach some understanding, of the situation in which they found themselves. So often, I felt that all I could do was to offer them, in spite of my best efforts, religion.

Three patients in particular, whom I still remember, helped to clear my mind on this point. One was a lady who was extremely religious. On her bedside locker she had a cross, various prayer books, pictures of the saints, and more besides. The whole surface of her locker was covered with religious bits and pieces. The outward observance of her religion was all to her. Try as I might, I could not move her on to talk in spiritual terms about her illness, the effect it was having upon her, upon her faith, and upon her relationship with God. By contrast, another lady I met aspired to no religious faith or outlook; she referred to herself merely as a "lapsed Anglican". But she was a woman of deep spirituality, and her funeral, which paradoxically she asked me to take, was one of the most deeply moving spiritual experiences in which I have ever been involved. Though the name of God was never once mentioned, I felt that we had moved beyond the barrier of religion into a spirituality in which I, at least, felt aware of God's presence in a way in which I felt strangely comfortable.

The third patient was an elderly lady who was dying of cancer. For me, she held the two previous extremes together and in balance. I went to see her at the request of her parish priest who told me she had only days to live. She thanked me for visiting, but told me very graciously and peaceably that she had been anointed by her own priest, received Holy Communion, and now felt ready to meet her Maker in her own way and in her own time. I asked to be allowed at least to pray with her, thanked God for our brief meeting, and went on my way rejoicing at her evident spirituality. I felt that even though she was dying, she had ministered to me, rather than I to her.

I am grateful to these people, and to those like them, for leading me on in their own way, and enabling me to see something which I should have been aware of much earlier in my years of ministry. The Gospels point to how much time and energy Jesus expended trying to show the people that their traditional religious practices were not sufficient in themselves to provide a real awareness of God in their lives, or to develop a living relationship with him. At times, we sense a real feeling of exasperation in Jesus – will these people never learn, or take his words to heart? "Woe to you, scribes and Pharisees, hypocrites! For you are like whitewashed tombs, which on the outside look beautiful ... so you also on the outside look righteous to others, but inside you are full of hypocrisy and lawlessness." By contrast, Jesus is in the same degree sympathetic to the scribe who asked him a question, and then responded to Jesus "wisely". "You are not far from the kingdom of God," was Jesus' encouraging reply.

If our spirituality can bring us as far as that, we have reason to be content. Our later years give us the opportunity to look again at where we stand. Religion offers us much. We love our Church. Its liturgy is part of us, the familiarity of the service, the readings, the hymns. We appreciate hearing a thought-provoking, well-constructed sermon or homily as a part of our spiritual nourishment. We draw strength from being part of a worshipping community, gathered in an act of praise and worship to God. But we also know that we must move on from there. What has taken place must move us forward to deepen our spirituality and our understanding of God. This can be a positive contribution which, as senior members, we offer to the worshipping community to which we belong. In this way, we can continue to "work for the good of all, and especially those of the family of faith".

Lord Jesus Christ,
we give thanks for the Church which bears your
name,
for the familiarity of its weekly and yearly round,
for the support which it offers us,
and for the comfort which it brings.
Move us on, we pray, to deepen our life in the
spirit,
where we can seek you, find you, and know you,
and become part of that love which you share with
the Father,
in the unity of the Spirit, world without end.
Amen.

It's okay to be me

I have a small circle of men friends with whom I meet up from time to time. We have a beer together, exchange news and views, and generally put the world to rights. "Cheers!" we say as we raise our glasses and take the top off our pints. It doesn't mean much. It's just a kind of greeting, a social convention, an acknowledgement of our meeting together and a friendship shared. From there, its use has extended to become an expression of thanks or a farewell greeting. The word suffers from over-use, and has very little meaning left. For me this is a great shame, because "Cheers!" comes from an ancient root, and carries with it a wealth of meaning.

The word has its root in the Latin word "cor", meaning heart. In French this has developed into "coeur", and was one of the words the Normans brought to England with them in the conquest of 1066. Chaucer and Shakespeare knew and used the word in this sense. "What cheer?" their characters greet each other, meaning literally, "What is the state of your heart?" As we greet each other these days, we ask "How are you?" or "How are you feeling?" The King James version of the Bible also uses the word in its old sense. "Be of good cheer," Jesus tells the disciples, "I have overcome the world." These are words of *encouragement*, a word which again has the same root, and means, literally, putting someone in good heart. So we cheer on our football team, or, on a more personal level, we do our best to cheer someone up, by whatever means it may be, when we see that they are down, and in low spirits.

I found that much of my ministry was eventually spent in this area of life. "Encouragement" somehow seems a poor-quality word to describe my pastoral concern, yet I can find no other, and that is exactly what I was trying to do, in the real and best sense of the word. I was not being facile by suggesting that if we were only to look on the bright side, difficulties would disappear, and everything would turn out for the best. My basic premise was that if we could be open and honest enough with ourselves and with God, we would find the acceptance, affirmation, and – that word again – encouragement that we need. In my days as a hospital chaplain, this was true of patients, relatives and staff. I was doing what I could to put them in good heart to face, day by day, a stressful situation. It was a case of being true to the real meaning of encouragement.

It is important to be in good heart at every stage of life, not least in our third age. Medical research suggests that when we are in good spirits we function well and consult our doctor less.

In other words, we are in good health. So being in good heart and good health are closely related. We enjoy an inner harmony, as it were, an inner reconciliation with ourselves, who we are and what we are. The voice within us is saying firmly and confidently, "Life is okay, and it's okay to be me." Being okay does not depend on our daily work and the status which that brings. Instead, we find the esteem and acceptance we need in God, who accepts us as we are, a mixture of the good, the bad and the incomprehensible.

This belief is fundamental to my faith. Yet there are many people who find it difficult, if not impossible, to accept or even begin to get their minds round the idea of the wideness of God's mercy and love, as the old hymn puts it. Is this, I wonder, because they do not love themselves in the first place? If people are not in good heart, if they are not at one with themselves, to what degree are they able to love the people around them? It seems to me that we are able to love other people only in proportion as we love ourselves, not in a selfish or self-centred kind of way, but knowing that we are loved by God, and that all love stems from God. I was taught my first verse from the Bible by our evangelical teacher just a day or two after I started school. It was 1 John 4:19, and the reference and the words I have never forgotten – how clearly I remember things from those far-off days: "We love him, because he first loved us" (KJV). It is this inner knowledge, or its outward expression of faith, that puts me, and keeps me, in good heart in my third age.

Later life is a time for personal fulfilment, positive enjoyment and reflection, all qualities which are life-enhancing. We have the opportunity to set out again in new directions, pursue new interests, try out new skills, develop new ideas, discover a new awareness of God's presence in our lives. So we can be in good heart, and take with us the words of David to his son Solomon: "Be strong and of good courage, and act. Do not be afraid or dismayed; for the Lord God, my God, is with you. He will not fail you or forsake you."

> *Heavenly Father,*
> *we give thanks*
> *that your presence has been with us across the*
> *years,*
> *and brought us now to later life. May we be in*
> *good heart*
> *knowing we are accepted and affirmed by those*
> *whom we know and love,*
> *and by the love made known to us*
> *in your Son, Jesus Christ our Lord. Amen.*

Forgiving ourselves

There is a kind of article which appears across a range of news-papers and magazines. The author is often a young mother trying to cope with the strains and stresses of family life. She seems to be constantly in a whirl, and perpetually harassed. Chaos reigns. The young mother is always facing conflict, either with the family, or within herself. She has no time for herself. The children take advantage of her because they know her weaknesses and how to manipulate her, so she is thoroughly disorganised. Her husband or partner seems totally unsympathetic to the state she is in, and only adds to it by his lack of interest, and by distancing himself from the situation. Everything that can go wrong seems to go wrong most of the time, certainly enough to provide the requisite number of words and fill the stipulated column inches week by week.

Days when it seems that everything that can go wrong does go wrong happen at every stage of life. We can allow ourselves to be amused by the young mother journalist telling us of her troubles and apparent failures. We can identify with her, and she engages a sympathetic response within us. Many of us can look back at the pressures of when we were young, whether we raised a family or not, and indulge them with a sympathetic smile.

We are far less sympathetic towards ourselves when things go wrong. There are days when we just miss buses, and the next one fails to arrive. And spectacles can be a constant source of frustration and irritation. Panic really set in one day when I was drawing out cash and the machine swallowed my card and simply died before my eyes. I cannot describe my relief, still standing there a few moments later and wondering what to do, when a door opened and a man emerged with my card in his hand. The look on my face must have immediately identified for him who the card belonged to. But as well as specific incidents such as these, there are days when, for whatever reason, I feel uncoordinated. My brain and my body seem unable or unwilling to engage with eachother. I know the signs. I know the feelings. It is very frustrating, and as a result, I feel cross and irritable. But instead of being angry with ourselves we should be doing just the opposite. We need to forgive ourselves.

Forgiveness is by no means a straightforward process. It is complicated and has many components. Between people, it involves an acknowledgement of what has taken place, and of the resultant hurt and pain that are placing great strain on the relationship. It also involves an acknowledgement of the feelings of guilt on one side, of blame on the other, and the consequent anger and hostility on both sides. The same elements are still present, even when no one else is involved, and we are doing battle with ourselves. Within us there is a conflict between nature and nurture, between what we are and what we have been conditioned to be. When we have a "bad day", part of us is saying, "It doesn't matter, these things happen. It's part of life, especially getting older." The other part of us is saying, "Of course it matters. You're only making excuses. You should be more careful. You've only got yourself to blame." The only means of avoiding being pulled apart in this way is for our inner voice to offer us the forgiveness that we need, and our inner self to accept it graciously. It is the way to reconciliation with, and wholeness within, ourselves.

The New Testament presents us with the person of Jesus, who by his dying and rising brings us forgiveness, and restores our broken relationship with God. In the words of St Paul: "Christ Jesus came into the world to save sinners." Our calling as Christians is therefore quite clear. We are to extend to one another the forgiving love that Christ offers to us, "forgiving one another, as God in Christ has forgiven you," to quote St Paul again. This message is central to the

Lord's Prayer: "Forgive us our sins, for we ourselves forgive everyone indebted to us." It does not, however, say anything about forgiving ourselves, which we also need.

Nevertheless, those words do point us in the right direction. As he writes to the Church at Rome, Paul uses this phrase: "Owe no one anything, except to love one another." Sometimes, in our more perceptive rather than self-centred moments, we find ourselves saying, "I owe it to myself ..." We owe it to ourselves to love ourselves, for our own sake, and as part of our Christian duty under God. This thought can be seen as being confirmed by some words of Jesus himself. Quoting the Jewish Law he said, "You shall love your neighbour as yourself." He was surely here confirming the very right and proper respect and love that we should have for ourselves as those who are made in the image of God. His only observation was that we should love other people just as much. Surely it must be that we can only love and nurture others in proportion as we have learned to love and respect ourselves. We need to extend that love and care and forgiveness to ourselves not only on "one of those days", but on every day that God grants us to live.

> *"Drop thy still dews of quietness,*
> *Till all our strivings cease;*
> *Take from our souls the strain and stress,*
> *And let our ordered lives confess*
> *The beauty of thy peace."* Amen.

Senior moments

I am sure most of us are familiar with the old joke about the minister visiting one of his senior church members. "Now that you are getting on in years," he says to her, "I think you would find it helpful to start thinking more about the hereafter." "Oh, but I do," she replies. "I'm always going upstairs or into another room and thinking to myself, 'Now what is it I'm here after?'"

We are only too familiar with the feeling and the situation. For no apparent reason, our minds just go blank without any warning, and we cannot remember what it was we were going to do next. Or perhaps we forget where we put things. How many times a day do we play Hunt the Glasses? And there is nothing worse than tidying things away, and putting them in a safe place – it is anyone's guess as to when and if we shall find them again. It happens to us all. That is bad enough, even though we can usually manage to laugh at ourselves, and keep the situation in perspective. It is more disconcerting when we are in the middle of saying something, and find we have lost the thread of what we were talking about, the point we started from, and the point we wanted to make. In a similar way, we repeat ourselves, the same opinions, the same expressions, the same stories. The trouble is that we fail to realise it, and it is other people who do. Our nearest and dearest are usually the ones to point out the truth to us. No matter how gently they do it, the truth can sometimes be painful.

Probably, the most disconcerting moments are those when we meet people we know well, or reasonably well, but unexpectedly, and we find that we simply cannot remember their names. Try as we might, we just cannot recall them, and the more we try, the more they elude us. Usually, the names we were trying to remember come back later, but that is no use for the present moment. There is not much choice as to how we handle the situation. Either we brazen it out, and hope we get away with it, which is a risky course of action to take, or we have to admit to our lapse of memory, make our apologies, and hope that we are forgiven. Such is the price of the third age.

But there are other senior moments of rather different kinds. There are times when memories come sweeping back and overwhelm us. They can be happy and delightful, as we recall moments which gave us pleasure. They can also be painful and sad, as we recall things from the past which we regret, and which still have their imprint on our lives today.

There is a holiday snap in our family collection taken of me when I was about six. My parents had called to me that it was time to leave the beach, and I was refusing to come. I looked cross, truculent, angry. My face must have been a picture, the reason, I am sure, for the photograph being taken. It was an early exercise for me in having to deal with the unreasonableness of one's parents, and the unfairness of life. It is disconcerting to find, some seventy years later, that when life appears to treat me unfairly, the angry child is still there inside me, kicking and stamping his feet, protesting at the unreasonableness of the situation he is in, and, as it were, refusing to come off the beach. As we grow older, and the amount of emotional energy at our disposal gets less, it can become more difficult to contain those old feelings. Words such as cantankerous, querulous, or just plain grumpy, come to mind.

However, it would be wrong to imply that senior moments are wholly negative. They can be awkward to deal with, but they can also tell us something about the nature of God. The opening chapters of Genesis give us the picture of a creator who organises the world in defined packages, everything tying in neatly together.

But we recognise that our world does not work in that way. There is no immutable pattern, there are no rigidly fixed lines. There is a randomness of which we are aware, but which we are unable to explain. This is part of the mystery of God.

In their own way, senior moments are part of the mystery of growing older. Their unpredictability can be difficult to cope with, and can even cause us embarrassment. Perhaps we worry too much. Senior moments remind us that life itself is unpredictable, as God, despite being constant, can also be unpredictable. This is the paradox with which we live as Christian people. As we grow older, we can have confidence to share our senior moments with God, and find God's acceptance and presence within them.

> *Eternal Father,*
> *we lay before you*
> *those moments in our lives*
> *which remind us*
> *of the passage of time.*
> *Reassure us with the knowledge*
> *that whatever our age,*
> *we are always your children.*
> *Make your loving presence known*
> *through all the changes and chances of life,*
> *and lead us to be one with you. Amen.*

What's in a name?

Norman Long was an artiste popular during the 1930s and early 1940s. He recited monologues which he accompanied himself at the piano. As well as appearing in the music halls and broadcasting in variety shows on the wireless, he made a number of records. We had one, which played frequently on our wind-up gramophone. It was called "Smythe, S-M-Y-T-H-E". It began "What's in a name? / You may hear folks exclaim, / Well some names don't matter a jot..." Later came the lines which I remember most clearly, even now, and for obvious reasons!

"In a person called Smith
Good taste is a myth.
Such a person prefers Brighton to Hove.
But just substitute y
for that third letter i,
and then tack on an e – and By Jove!
Then it's Smythe, S-M-Y-T-H-E,
it goes with those blazers we see … "

So then, what's in a name? There may be a lot, and it may be more important than we think, or than first meets the eye. Take my family, for example. There is a quirk in that my father, my brother and I have all been called by our last Christian name. My father and brother seemed to manage reasonably well, only having two, but I have three, and that has always presented me with some difficulty. I have never been sure how to sign myself, and in a minor kind of way, have always suffered something of an identity crisis. Over recent years, this has been compounded – or perhaps now simplified – by official lists on computers which seem only able to cope with two names. So increasingly now, I am having to use

Charles, my first name, which I am getting used to, and quite like. Neville is my third name, so often gets omitted. I have no problem with this, as I have never really liked the name that much. Perhaps the last straw was when my namesake became the archetypal naughty boy in one of Joyce Grenfell's delightful sketches. In a beautiful piece of understatement, as a fraught schoolteacher faced with losing control of her class, she exclaimed in the classic line, "Neville, don't do that!"

In a subtle and indefinable way, we grow into our names. They represent us to the people round about us, and with whom we come into contact on a daily basis. Our names communicate our personalities, who we are, and what we are. In some way, they characterise us. So I suppose it would cause other people some kind of confusion as far as I am concerned, if I were suddenly to become Charles instead of Neville, or the more familiar Nev.

The idea of growing into one's name contrasts with the biblical idea of giving a name with a definite meaning, and for a particular purpose. Thus when God appeared to Abram and announced that he would become through God's covenant "the ancestor of a multitude of nations", he renamed him Abraham, which conveyed exactly that meaning. The four children of the prophet Hosea fared less well. Their father gave them all names denoting God's approaching judgement on the people of Israel.

The importance of a child's name in Jewish tradition and culture is emphasised by the first chapter of St Luke's Gospel. First we read of the miraculous conception of a child by Elizabeth and Zechariah. "I am an old man," protested Zechariah to the angel who brought him the news, "and my wife is getting on in years." The angel would have no argument: "You will name him John." This was vitally important. The child was not to be called Zechariah after his father, according to custom, but to bear a totally different name which meant "the gift of God". A parallel announcement by the angel to Mary heralded another unexpected conception of a male child. "You shall name him Jesus," instructed the angel, a name which Matthew, in the birth narrative at the beginning of his Gospel, explains for us. "You are to name him Jesus, for he will save his people from their sins." Matthew regards the event as the fulfilment of Old Testament prophecy, and provides us with a second significant name for the child: "The virgin shall conceive and bear a son and they shall call him Emmanuel, which means 'God is with us'."

In my later years, I cannot think but that some very strange names are being settled upon for our children. They are names which appear to be made up at whim, and to have very little meaning or shape or purpose. They do not even sound elegant or pleasing on the ear, an observation which shows my age, my conservative attitude, and how out of touch I am with the rising generation. Nevertheless, I do wonder how these names will sound when the people who bear them are no longer young. Even more seriously, I also wonder whether a person can "grow into" a made-up name of this kind. We hear much about our young people indulging in bad behaviour because they lack self-esteem. Perhaps it could be that a person's perception of themselves, and their sense of self-esteem, is adversely affected by the kind of name they bear.

However, even though fashions in names come and go, many names have stood the test of time, and are still popular. Indeed, some of the Old Testament names seem to be making a comeback. Infant baptism is in decline, yet naming ceremonies have become important family occasions, especially where the parents are not married. The naming ceremony then becomes a kind of public declaration that the family unit has been established by the arrival of the child. I recognise that this is not church orthodoxy, but it is life as it is lived in the early twenty-first century. I like to believe that when Jesus said, "Let the little children come to me; do not stop them", he did not add any conditions about parentage or families. He simply added, "For it is to such as these that the kingdom of God belongs." Whatever we may think or feel about it, a name is a name, and by that name we are known to God. "I have called you by name, you are mine," says the Lord.

Almighty Father,
you know us as we are,
and by the names we bear.
Make us your own
by your calling,
so that we may know you and serve you,
and one another for your sake,
in the name of Jesus Christ,
your Son, our Lord. Amen.

Self-esteem

I still have a vivid recollection of a service I took many years ago now. After the blessing at the end, I went to the main door to greet people on their way out. As I shook hands with them and introduced myself, so they told me who they were. A pattern seemed to emerge: "I'm just a shop assistant ... a working mum ... a housewife ... I'm retired now." It was all so apologetic, and I found it strangely odd. I could not recall having come across anything similar in any of the various churches in the area where I live, and where I helped out from time to time. I knew the parish priest reasonably well, and felt that he was the last person to load his people with heavy demands and unrealistic expectations that they could not live up to in the expression of their faith. On the contrary, I felt sure that he would have encouraged them to be themselves, and to bring their various gifts and talents to fruition within a Christian context. "By the grace of God," wrote St Paul, "I am what I am." Our self-esteem is rooted and grounded in that short phrase. God knows us, loves us, accepts us, as we are and for what we are.

Nevertheless, the question of self-esteem may be one which we have to deal with in later life. So many of our feelings of self-worth are bound up not only with who we are, and what we are, but with what we do, with our occupation. "Post-retirement depression" is a recognised problem which affects many people when they retire. So much of our sense of well-being, our sense of status, our sense of purpose, has been bound up for so many years in the work we have done, in the job we have performed. When we move beyond that, no matter how carefully we prepare for retirement, the gap may be difficult to fill. That is why so many of us become involved in voluntary activities of all kinds. Of course we want to get out of the house and have a good reason for doing so. Of course we want to meet other people. We find their company stimulating, and in this way we make new friends. Of course we want to share news and views and common interests. Of course we want to feel we are contributing to a good cause, as indeed we are. (It would be fascinating to know how many "volunteer hours" are contributed over the whole country over the course of a year. The figure, I am sure, would be staggering.) All these reasons generate, and add to, our feeling of personal self-esteem. But I guess that our greatest reason for feeling good is that we are engaged in an activity which is worthwhile in itself, even if it is unremunerated. There lies the feel-good factor in our later years. There lies the basis of our self-esteem.

My only concern is that the movement is entirely outwards. We need to base our self-esteem not only on doing, outwardly, but on being, inwardly. This is especially important for those who, for one reason or another, are not able to engage in "outside activities", or feel that such activities are not for them, in order to establish a foundation and a direction for their self-esteem. We can find the validation which we need, and seek for, within our Christian faith. In the Gospels, we find people hesitating to approach Jesus because their self-esteem, and perception of self-worth, is so low. The woman who had been suffering from haemorrhages for twelve years was ritually unclean and socially unacceptable because of her condition. She approached Jesus, neither wanting nor daring to do any more than to touch just the fringe of his cloak, believing that if she did, she would be made well. When this happened, and Jesus called her out of the crowd, "she came in fear and trembling". His words healed her in body and mind, and restored her self-esteem: "Go in peace, and be healed." Jesus saw his ministry as the fulfilment of the Old Testament prophecy of Isaiah: "To bring good news to the poor … to let the oppressed go free." We do not, I hope, lessen the powerful social thrust of this message by applying it equally to those who are poor in spirit or feel themselves inwardly oppressed.

It is vital that our sense of self-esteem should be in good order in our later years, so that our lives should continue to have meaning and purpose for as long as possible. When the time comes that our inward strength and sense of purpose begin to wane, we still have the episode of blind Bartimaeus to encourage us, even though we may still retain our sight. Bartimaeus is a forlorn figure, sitting by the roadside begging, on the fringes of society because of his affliction. When Jesus comes by, Bartimaeus begins to call out to him, but many in the crowd sternly order him to be quiet. Jesus does take notice, however, and the crowd alters its tone: "Take heart ... he is calling you." We too can take heart. That call of Jesus carries with it the affirmation we need in our later years, and encourages our self-esteem.

> *Father, we lay before you*
> *our need for personal affirmation,*
> *and our search for self-esteem.*
> *We give thanks for the activities*
> *which we can now offer freely*
> *in the time available to us,*
> *and for the sense of purpose*
> *they bring us.*
> *Above all, may we know*
> *that we are loved and accepted*
> *through your Son, Jesus Christ,*
> *and truly valued in his love. Amen.*

The body

I have come to recognise that I am now much more aware of my body than I used to be. This must be one of the symptoms of the third age. When I was young and at work, I was never really aware of it. My body and I were one. It was rather like a friend of mine who is a superb driver. His car does whatever he wants it to, and expresses his will at the merest touch. So my body took me where I wanted, and my personality found its expression in my body language, as it is now popularly known. I knew my body needed occasional maintenance, but I could do this with a minimum of effort, and apart from the odd minor ailment, I was able to take my robust good health very much for granted.

I am extremely thankful that I am still in good health. It would be an exaggeration to say that my body and I have grown apart since I entered the third age, but I am aware that there is no longer the seamless expression of oneness that once existed between us. I am aware that an increased degree of maintenance is required. I make more visits to the GP to check for this, or consult for that. I now need some low-level medication, so I make another visit to the surgery before I receive another prescription and so I have come to be known and recognised at my local pharmacy.

Organisations and institutions as well as people also suffer from the ageing process. The Church is no exception, and shows signs of wear and tear from its two thousand years of continued existence. In his letter to the Colossians, Paul writes of Christ as "the head of the body, the Church". For Paul, this is a crucial and recurring theme. "Just as the body is one and has many members, and all the members of the body, though many, are one body, so it is with Christ." So it must have been extremely painful for him to have

71

visited Corinth only to find that there were quarrels and disputes between the Christians in that city, with conflicting loyalties and division into rival factions. This same sad story has continued down the years, causing enormous harm to the Church as the Body of Christ here on earth. However, I like to believe that under the guidance of the Spirit, and with much goodwill and openness on the part of its members, the Church can regenerate itself. The process of dying and rising which Christ accomplished in his own body is crucial to our understanding of the Gospel message and of our own calling as Christian people. It is a process which is preserved and personalised for each one of us as we receive the sacrament of the Eucharist.

The New Testament speaks to us also of the importance of the bodily presence of Christ. Born in the poorest of circumstances, and raised in obscurity, Jesus emerged into the drama of political and religious life when he was baptised by John in the Jordan. This event was followed by his forty days in the wilderness, with the testing both of body and spirit which it brought him. His rough, nomadic ministry, preaching and teaching then ensued, which made stern demands on his physical as well as spiritual and emotional stamina. This path inevitably led him to Jerusalem and the brutality inflicted on his body there. As Jesus journeyed to the eventual breaking of his own body, he healed the bodies of many who came to him in need of physical help and personal wholeness. Perhaps one might tell the story of Jesus' ministry in terms of his body and physical presence.

Perhaps, too, we might tell the story of our own lives in a similar way. We are conscious, sometimes painfully so, of what our bodies once were, and what we have become. Inevitably, there is a degree of loss, a feeling of sadness. Whatever medication my GP may prescribe for me, I know that it will not and cannot reverse the ageing process. But, in the words of St Paul, "I do not lose heart."

I thank God that my body has served me well and brought me to my later years. Now I seek to nurture it as much as possible, be gentle with it, forgive it for what it is no longer able to do, and have the patience and forbearance to live within these limitations. Ultimately, I must trust that as a member of the body of Christ, my own body bears the pattern of his dying and rising.

Father Creator,
we give thanks
for the bodies you have given to us,
and which have supported and sustained us
across the years.
As their strength declines
in later life,
may our faith be strong to know
that our bodies bear within them
the pattern of the dying and rising
of your Son, Jesus Christ our Lord. Amen.

Dissonance in life

There is a very real part of me that would like to be able to regard my faith as a harmonious whole. It would be a simplistic approach, based on the Bible in its entirety, as a source of affirmation and inspiration, a guide to dealing with all the stresses and problems of life. I would like to see it as a guidebook for sorting out the tangle of relationships which can leave us feeling perplexed and exhausted.

I have to realise that the reality is rather different. The Bible presents us with very real feelings of disharmony and discord – of dissonance. The Old Testament contains details of bloody battles, of wars and personal violence, of political alliances and subsequent treacheries. Such parts can be distinctly unedifying, while it can be extremely tedious to read the detailed provisions of the Jewish Law. The psalms speak of great faith in the loving presence of God, contrasted with expressions of great frustration and anger because of the apparent failure of God's promises towards the chosen people. The prophets sometimes tell of justice and retribution, sometimes of peace and restoration. In the New Testament, some of St Paul's letters scold the converts in the churches which he has founded, while others wax lyrical with enthusiasm and encouragement for his new Christians.

Dissonance is woven into the thread of the Gospel story. Mary and Joseph take the infant Jesus to the Temple in Jerusalem. They need to make the ritual offering laid down in Jewish law, "a pair of turtle-doves or two small pigeons". More than that, their hearts are full. They want to express their gratitude for the safe delivery of their first-born in circumstances which, according to St Luke, were distinctly unfavourable. But what should have been a moment of rejoicing becomes ominous. The aged Simeon prophesies to Mary, "A sword will pierce your own soul too". The words were echoed years later when Jesus said to his disciples, "Do not think I have come to bring peace on earth. I have not come to bring peace but a sword." In a sense, the sword hovered again over Jesus' relationships with his own family when he appeared to be very stern with them, even to the point of rejection: "Whoever does the will of God is my brother and sister and mother." Where we expect to find family harmony, instead we find dissonance. It is disconcerting to realise that this dissonance lies at the heart of the Gospel message. God becomes human through virgin birth. God's glory is expressed through the way Jesus identifies with his fellow beings and serves them. His life ends with the degradation of public crucifixion, yet the process of death was reversed on the third day. The whole Christian faith is based on paradox, on contradiction, on dissonance.

It is no surprise, therefore, to realise that dissonance is an integral part of our lives, at any stage of life, but perhaps especially so in our later years. We may contrast what we once were with what we are now, the ambitions and hopes we once cherished with what we were actually able to achieve. We may find a frustrating imbalance between what we can do, and what we would like to be able to do. There may be a dissonance between knowing that we have many more years behind us than ahead of us, and knowing how best to use the time still available to us. There are all kinds of conflicting feelings and jarring emotions between the people we are, and the people we would like to be. So I am always encouraged by a verse from St Paul's letter to the Romans: "I do not do the good I want, but the evil I do not want is what I do." In these words, he recognises the dissonance within himself, and in his relationship with other people. It is the dissonance found at the heart of the Gospel. It resonates profoundly within me, and perhaps within us all.

I remember going to see an exhibition of paintings by a local artist. Most of them were of still-life, and, I have to say, much of a muchness. The best painting by far in the exhibition was an abstract. The artist had really let himself go. There was colour, there was life. There was more vitality in that one painting than in the rest of the exhibition put together. The artist had stumbled on the discovery, like so many before him, together with poets, musicians and writers, that dissonance can be a positive quality. It leads us to a deeper recognition that this may be the way in which God is revealed. We are confronted with the paradox that, through dissonance, we are brought into harmony with God.

> *Lord God our Creator,*
> *who at the beginning of time*
> *brought order out of chaos,*
> *enable us to find you*
> *within the dissonance of our lives,*
> *so that we may cope with the demands*
> *of change and contradiction,*
> *knowing that both*
> *are at the heart of the faith*
> *that you have set before us*
> *in your Son, Jesus Christ our Lord. Amen.*

Life is an enigma

In a wireless broadcast to the nation on 1 October 1939, Winston Churchill declared in his characteristically pugnacious tones: "I cannot forecast to you the action of Russia. It is a riddle, wrapped in a mystery, inside an enigma." We have seen in the years since how right that observation was. It was not only one of Churchill's masterly turns of phrase, it was a shrewdly accurate guess as to Russia's underlying intent and purpose during the war; not only a desperate struggle to protect the fatherland, but to extend the boundaries of communism as far as was politically possible. It was only recently that European frontiers were restored to something like they were sixty or seventy years ago, a time which increasingly few of us can remember with any degree of accuracy. Since then, there have been many enigmatic politicians. Stalin was by no means the only one, and, as we look around, the situation appears to have changed very little. Public life and leadership at all levels present us with many enigmas.

So, unfortunately, does our faith. On various occasions recorded in the Gospels, Jesus seems to have been more than a little enigmatic. "Son of Man" was a title that he frequently used of himself. Scholars have pondered long and hard, and written learned books, about the significance of the title, and the implications of what it might mean. The enigma has never been satisfactorily explained, or fully understood. Nor has it ever been entirely clear as to whether Jesus intended to found what we know as the Church. The Gospels record his parting words to the disciples, sending them out in his name to preach, to teach and to heal, but we cannot know for sure whether Jesus had in mind to establish a recognisable body of believers who would bear and perpetuate his name. It is an enigma with which we have to live as part of our faith.

We can find this difficult, and it is at least some consolation to know that at times the disciples did too. In St John's Gospel, Jesus, with his impending death, resurrection and ascension in mind, says to his disciples: "A little while, and you will no longer see me, and again a little while, and you will see me." This enigmatic remark baffles the disciples. We can sense the bewilderment growing, and the sense of frustration rising: "We do not know what he is talking about." They are just longing for Jesus to speak plainly to them, and they are very relieved later on in the same chapter when this eventually happens: "Now you are speaking plainly, not in any figure of speech!" Generally, however, it is Jesus' custom to leave it to the disciples to hear his words, and to work out the meaning for themselves. So Matthew tells us: "Jesus told the crowds these things in parables; without a parable he told them nothing." On the other hand Mark says that Jesus "explained everything in private to his disciples."

We might well wish that we were able to take advantage of this explanation, especially if Jesus were talking about the end of life and what lies beyond. This is the enigma that still confronts us in our third age. If only we knew what to expect, we might be able to prepare ourselves more fully, or even just prepare ourselves a little. But Jesus appears to say that he is unable to help us on this point. Indeed, it is beyond his power to do so. When the disciples anxiously ask him, just before his ascension, about the future and what is likely to happen to them, Jesus replies firmly: "It is not for you to know the times or the periods which the Father has set by his own authority." It was enough that the disciples should be faithful witnesses to Jesus "in Jerusalem, in all Judea and Samaria, and to the ends of the earth".

On the face of it, that is another enigmatic reply. Yet as we consider its implications, we begin to see that it relieves us of a lot of unnecessary anxiety about what lies ahead and what may eventually happen to us. It seems to be saying that God has given us our life. It is sufficient to get on and live it to the full for as long as we can. Life itself is an enigma. Perhaps we shall only fully understand when we come to pass through the greatest enigma of all.

Father,
we lay before you
the enigma of our lives,
and the final enigma of our death.
Give us grace to live our lives
to the full until their end,
and faith to leave to you
the unfolding of the last enigma
when we enter into your presence
and find that all will be revealed. Amen.

Half-empty, or half-full?

Such is the classic illustration of the contrast between a pessimist and an optimist. One looks at the situation from a negative point of view, the other regards it positively. Another colourful way of expressing the difference in attitudes is that an optimist will say, "Pass the cream", while the pessimist asks, "Is there any milk?"

I must admit to writing these words with a certain degree of feeling, since my own personal predisposition is towards pessimism rather than optimism. I am not sure whether my inherent pessimism comes from nature or nurture – a bit of both, I suspect – but it has always been something of a family joke, and over the years they have, by and large, laughed me out of it. I recognise that I have this pessimistic streak which is part of me and won't go away. But I can live with it, it does not trouble me, and I can usually manage to recognise it and see the funny side. I can also respond genuinely to the idea that life is for living. We have only one life. In our third age, we realise increasingly that time is limited, so we should live life to the full and appreciate as fully as we can the many blessings it brings. Jesus said that he came to bring us life, life in all its fullness. In enjoying the fullness of life – physically, emotionally, spiritually – we are partaking in the Christ's resurrection. It is his gift of eternal life which he shares with all those who believe in him. All that, I believe and gladly subscribe to.

So it comes as something of a jolt to the positive outlook on life that I have yearned after and striven for over the years to read a report of some research that suggests pessimism, maybe, is not such a bad thing after all. A touch of pessimism, the report suggested, enables people to take control of their lives, and order them better than those who are optimists. Pessimists cope better with stress, and because they are used to handling negative feelings, they make better listeners for other people.

There is much food for thought there. It set me thinking again about the person of Jesus as portrayed in the Gospels. He seems to have lived life to the full, as a member of the family, as a craftsman in the family business, and as an itinerant preacher. We are not told of any close relationship, but a single status does not mean, as many will testify, that life is unfulfilled or unfulfilling. Within the three or four years of his public ministry, Jesus packed in a wealth of experience that has sustained and inspired his followers for over two thousand years. He did not allow himself to be carried away by any unreal optimism in his enthusiasm for the kingdom of God. His mission is grounded in earthly – and, on occasion, earthy – reality. He does not indulge in other-worldly piety. His optimism is expressed through enabling others to realise their hidden potential. Any unreal optimism that Jesus may have entertained as he emerged into the public eye was immediately punctured by his experience of the three temptations, his time of testing in the desert. Through them, he learned where his true destiny lay.

In the light of the report which I read about, perhaps those events had a greater and more lasting effect on Jesus than we realise. We tend to think of them, and perhaps to isolate them, as belonging to the beginning of Lent. Lent presents us with a busy calendar of events to think about in the life of Jesus, and we quickly pass on to other aspects of his ministry, and the events leading up to Holy Week and Easter. But we notice time and again in the Gospels what a good listener Jesus was, both to Jews and Gentiles, and to people of every description and of every social class. We notice, too, that Jesus retained a significant degree of control over events leading to his crucifixion. Perhaps there was more within him of the pessimist than we realise, or even dare to attribute to him. Nevertheless, we are left with the picture of a balanced personality, someone who managed to hold the conflicting elements of his inner self in equilibrium. The only time Jesus wavers is in the Garden of Gethsemane, when the burden of events weighs too heavily upon him, and he feels momentarily overwhelmed: "Father, if you are willing, remove this cup from me." Just as quickly, he recovers his poise: "Yet not my will, but yours, be done." He moves on from Gethsemane to face his death with resolution and calmness.

That same balance is important for us. Few of us are wholly optimists, few wholly pessimists. Most of us are a mixture. We carry within us elements of both extremes, and have moments when we swing in one direction rather than the other. Overall, we need to maintain a healthy balance. Perhaps in our third age, it does not matter too much whether the cup is half-empty or half-full. What does matter is that we make the most of the life that God has given to us, and enjoy it in all its fullness.

Lord, you are about us and within us,
and know us better than we know ourselves.
Enable us to see
that as you create us in your image,
and sustain us in your love,
we can accept every part of our being,
and find our peace and wholeness in you. Amen.

Digging the garden

I thought I had a good idea for a section in this book. It was going to be called "The Garden". It took as its starting point the remarkable growth in the popularity of gardening over the last few years. Gardening is now big business, as a visit to almost any garden centre will confirm. Thousands of people flock to Chelsea and the other major garden shows. All this activity is reflected in the number of gardening magazines and gardening programmes on radio and television, and the celebrities they have produced.

My idea went on to point out the important setting provided by gardens in the Bible. In one of the Genesis stories in the Old Testament, the drama of creation takes place in the Garden of Eden. Its peace and harmony are soon shattered by the temptation and disobedience of Adam and Eve, and their expulsion from the garden. The climax to the New Testament is approached through the events in the Garden of Gethsemane. Jesus, too, was tempted, but he was not deflected from the path that led to the death he was to endure in Jerusalem. He left the garden under arrest, and events moved quickly to his trial and crucifixion. His body was removed from the cross, and placed in a garden tomb. It was there that the resurrection took place. Jesus appeared to Mary Magdalene who thought that he was the gardener. So my point was going to be that our activity in the garden across the seasons mirrors the pattern of death and resurrection which takes place in the gardens of the Bible and brings us close to God. This was a train of thought that I had worked out for myself. I had not read it anywhere or heard it set out before. I was really quite pleased with what I thought was my original idea. So I was more than a little deflated to be sitting in the congregation one Sunday soon afterwards, and hear the preacher use the same set of images and ideas. So much for my originality!

By this time the section had been written for the book, but rather than scrap my idea altogether, I began to think it through. As I did so, I realised that the preacher and I had both missed the vital point. It was understandable for him, because I know that he is not a gardener, whereas I like to think I am, at least to the extent that I find it therapeutic to get my hands dirty, and to get things to grow.

What I had overlooked is that a garden is never static. It is alive, always growing, always changing. Something is always moving, even in the depths of winter. So a garden needs tending and feeding. It needs to be cultivated and nurtured in order to bring out the best results. We need to keep working at it, if not necessarily digging, then at least turning the soil, in order to give it light and air and to keep it fresh. As a result of our efforts, there are times when we can relax and enjoy the garden that we have had the pleasure and fulfilment of creating. It is no coincidence that our word "paradise" comes from the old Persian word for garden. And so it is with ourselves. There are times to be at ease, to enjoy looking back on the way we have come, to take stock of where we are now, and to contemplate what might lie ahead. There are also times to be up and doing, active on God's behalf. "Are you still sleeping and taking your rest?" Jesus asked his disciples in the Garden of Gethsemane. "Get up, let us be going." There is work to be done, not just on our garden, but on ourselves as well. In later life, no less than at any other time, we need to go on growing in our awareness of God's presence with us, God's activity through us and around us.

> *Heavenly Father, we give thanks for all that grows*
> *and bears witness to the wonder of your handiwork*
> *in the process of creation and re-creation.*
> *In our later life, give us the strength of mind and spirit*
> *to dig deeply, and to discover the roots of your love*
> *made known to us in your Son, Jesus Christ our Lord.*
> *Amen.*

Ageing is not for softies

It is a disconcerting characteristic of the third age that memories come back, unexpectedly and unbidden. We may be absorbed in what we are doing, preoccupied with something apparently totally unconnected, when a memory, long forgotten and deeply buried in the past, suddenly floats to the surface of our consciousness, and claims our attention. We can find ourselves reliving the moment, experiencing the same feelings as we did long ago, seeing the event as we knew it, undiminished by the passage of time. Just for the moment, it is almost as if we are caught up in some kind of time warp.

This book had its origin in one such moment. As a young man, I belonged to the Round Table, a social organisation for fellowship and good works in the community for the under-forties. At one meeting, I was asked to propose a vote of thanks to the speaker. I was still young in the ministry at that time. My level of self-confidence was not high, especially when expected to say something in public off-the-cuff. I cannot now remember what the speaker had been talking about, but he was an older man, and he must have been reminiscing about his experiences, because he ended by quoting, by way of an apology, the words of the prophet Joel: "Your old men shall dream dreams, and your young men shall see visions." I gratefully seized on this Old Testament prophecy, and used it as the basis for my vote of thanks, so managing to avoid the usual platitudes. I linked his talk to his younger audience by saying that it was when old men dreamed dreams that young men saw visions.

I was pleased with my vote of thanks, and it may have sounded all right on the night. I expect that I am the only person who still remembers it, after all these years, but I do so not because it gives me pleasure, but because it reminds me of my callowness. I have lived long enough to realise how wrong I was. The dreams of the old no longer inspire the visions of the young, if indeed they ever did. The young move inexorably into a future which is increasingly divorced from the past. There is no longer what we used to call "a generation gap". That was a gentle and convenient expression by which the differing outlooks of varying ages or succeeding generations within a family could be accepted and absorbed without causing too much open disagreement. That may be no longer possible. We are confronted by a gap created by instant communication with anyone almost anywhere else in the world, yet which seems unable to bring with it a corresponding degree of understanding and meeting of minds. It is a gap which encompasses a different relationship to culture, language and history, a history to which we personally belong in later life. It can be odd to hear the events of our lifetime being taught or recounted as history in a way which we would not recognise or easily identify with. More disturbing, I find, is an apparent unawareness of history, and an inability or unwillingness to learn from history. It may be this, at least in part, which is leading us into the "wars and rumours of wars" which characterise the early years of the twenty-first century.

It can be disconcerting to move into later years, or to spend them against this disturbing background. We might well be tempted to echo the cry of the psalmist, "Even to old age and grey hairs, O God, do not forsake me." No amount of pre-retirement training courses can prepare us for the circumstances which surround us. Some words of Jesus, though not apparently specifically aimed at older people, have meaning for us. "No one sews a piece of unshrunk cloth on an old cloak ... neither is new wine put into old wineskins ... new wine is put into fresh wineskins ..." So at least no one is expecting us to be other than what we are. But I have to admit to an approving nod towards the comment on these words that seems to have crept into Luke's version: "No one after drinking old wine desires new wine, but says 'the old wine is good'". Those words are affirming and reassuring, as are those from the book of Joel which I quoted all those years ago: "I will pour out my Spirit on all flesh." The prophecy is all-inclusive. Sons and daughters, young and old, no one is to be missed. The dreams of the old, and the visions of the young, are all the gifts of God's Spirit. God is calling us as senior members of the community in general, and of the Church in particular, to engage with life, even when it seems to contradict so much of who we are and what we stand for, our standards and ideals, our beliefs and values: the qualities and, for us, realities which have sustained us over the years, and formed the framework of our lives.

We reflect, not in the sense of looking back all the time, or seeking to live in the past, but in order to use our experience of life to find meaning in the changes which surround us, and in which we are inevitably caught up. Perhaps we only really become old when we are unable or unwilling to do this any longer. But to persevere as long as we can in this direction brings us closer to the kingdom of heaven, which, said Jesus, "is like the master of a household who brings out of his treasure what is new, and what is old". It is not always easy being old, nor should we expect it to be. Ageing is not for softies.

Heavenly Father,
you have been with us
and guided us
on our path through life.
Be with us still in our later years
when we are confronted
by changing circumstances, outlooks and values,

conflicting with those
that have been part of us
and supported us across the years.
May your Spirit enable us
still to engage with life,
so that we may know ourselves
to be affirmed as the people we are,
with a place in your Church,
and a place in your kingdom,
where you include in your treasures
things both new and old,
now and for ever. Amen.

Personal space

The old chestnut still does the rounds. The wife remarks, somewhat irritably of her newly retired husband, "I married him for better or for worse – but not for lunch." We can still raise a smile when we hear the old joke repeated yet again, because we recognise the truth which it conveys. The wife is complaining that her husband is around the house, if not all the time, then at least a great deal more than he used to be when he was at work. He would go off in the morning, and not return until the evening. During that time, the house was hers, and her time was her own to arrange as she chose. Weekends and holidays were the time for the couple to be together, not all day and every day. Those of us who have passed through this stage, and got used to retirement, are well aware of dynamics and difficulties which can be involved in any relationship. We can afford to smile knowingly. But the smile may distance us from an uncomfortable truth, and help us to cope with it more easily.

Some years ago, my daughter took an allotment. It had not been cultivated for a long time, and was very much in need of care and attention. There was a greenhouse, which had more or less collapsed, but there was also a shed, which, although neglected, was still in reasonable condition. Inside, my daughter found shelves and hooks, and nails in the wall to hang tools from. More significantly, there was a bench with a padded seat, and an old paraffin stove of the kind that would boil a kettle as well as providing heat. A picture seemed to emerge of a man, probably retired, who spent much of his time there, on his allotment, with his greenhouse, growing his flowers and vegetables, and with the added convenience of his own shed, however humble, where he could sit and make his own drink, and keep warm in winter. In this way, he and his wife or partner both had their own space, and were able to maintain that space in a way that was satisfactory to each of them. Perhaps it was their way of dealing with a difficult, or potentially difficult situation.

It is not hard to see where difficulties and problems arise. Differences and contrasts in outlook and personality, that once were attractive and helped originally to bring a couple together, can in later life become irksome and a source of irritation. Both have equal claims upon the time and space which are available to them. Homemakers may feel that the area which they have always regarded as their own, at least for a substantial part of the day, is now being invaded, and protest accordingly. The fact that the invasion is being caused by the person closest to them only makes matters worse. Yet it is equally reasonable that the newly retired people will want to establish new boundaries of time and space, and will need to do this as they embark on a new stage of life. The only place that this can happen is the home. Major adjustments have to be made on both sides if many tensions, much resentment and mutual recrimination are to be avoided. Yet in later life, we find it more difficult to adjust. We shall never know whether the man with his allotment was using his shed to help him make that adjustment, or to avoid it altogether.

What characterises the relationship between people living closely together may be reflected in our religious life in later years. Inevitably, there has to be adjustment, and what once seemed attractive may become a source of irritation. So I find that it takes much patience and real effort to understand and adapt to changes in liturgy and the presentation of public worship. Language alters its meaning, and I find that the Gospel and the mission of the Church are now expressed in terms that I am not entirely clear about, or comfortable with. So I look in other directions to find space in which I can find a wider vision of God, and broaden and deepen my awareness of God. God works through the Church, but is not confined to it, or constrained by it. God "is able to accomplish abundantly far more than we can ask or imagine." So I find God speaks to me through the brush of a great painter, through the music I listen to, the books I read, the films I see. And not only in works of art. In so many strands of our daily life God is there, waiting to be discovered. The moment of discovery can be moving, overwhelming, deeply sacramental, a moment when we are "filled with all the fullness of God."

Moments like this, when we know we are close to and enriched by God's presence, need time and space. The relationships which we form, or re-form, with those who are closest to us as we grow older also need the time and space now available to us. We may realise new qualities within ourselves and within other people, which will grow and deepen those relationships vital to us, and which sustain us in our later years.

> *Eternal God, you entered our world*
> *in the person of your son.*
> *Enable us to use*
> *the time and space of later life*
> *to explore the expressions*
> *of your loving presence among us*
> *to enrich our lives,*
> *and our relationships with one another,*
> *and to deepen our faith*
> *in Jesus Christ our Lord. Amen.*

An attitude problem

I have to tell you that I have an attitude problem. I know because my neighbour told me. He was a man in his thirties who, with his partner some ten years younger, had rented the house next door. They had a baby, a delightful little girl, who was no problem at all. A major problem was his daughter by a previous partner who invited her friends and her friends' friends to climb the trees and ride their bikes over the common area of green in front of our row of houses. We were troubled by the volume and reverberations of his super hi-fi, and by the loud late-night parties in the back garden, where the conversation was coarse, and every other word, it seemed, had no more than four letters.

One day, it all came to a head over something completely trivial and unrelated. We had, as they say, a full and frank discussion of wide-ranging issues. Much as I hate confrontation, it was a useful thing to do, and the right thing to do. It cleared the air and our relationship was much better until they eventually left, leaving the house in a state of complete disarray. But my neighbour had the last word in our argument, and I shall always remember what he said: "The trouble with you, Neville, is that you've got an attitude problem." I shall remember his words, because, of course, he was absolutely right. I must have made it abundantly clear what my attitude was towards him, his friends, and his children's friends. No wonder my problem was plain to see.

Having spent my entire working life in a service occupation, I regard communication as a vital component of everyday life. A smile costs nothing, and makes the day seem brighter. A word of thanks or mutual appreciation helps along any transaction. I am not partial to being addressed as "mate" by a young male assistant. I am sure he is being friendly, and it may be the way he talks to his mates, but I am not one of them. If I feel someone is being friendly and helpful, and really trying to meet my needs, I am more likely to consult them again, or to pay a return visit to that shop. But I feel that carries very little weight or consideration these days, and that the concept of the satisfied customer is just an outmoded attitude that belongs to those of us in later life. Such are my thoughts as I stand in yet another slow-moving queue at the supermarket checkout!

So if I have an attitude problem, so do many other people. But none of this is new. Jesus spent much of his ministry challenging attitudes. "Woe to you, scribes and Pharisees!" was a phrase frequently on his lips. But he also challenged the attitudes of his disciples. They appear to have been slow to absorb the meaning of his stern words "If any want to become my followers, let them deny themselves and take up their cross and follow me." Instead we find them jostling for positions of rank and status in the new kingdom which featured so prominently in Jesus' teaching. James and John asked him, "Grant us to sit, one at your right hand and one at your left, in your glory." Perhaps they would even argue among themselves which of them would take the premier place. These were typical of the attitudes that Jesus was trying to change so that the disciples would understand his mission, the nature and purpose of his ministry, and be there when he needed them. One of the most poignant moments of the whole Gospel narrative takes place in the courtyard of the high priest, where Peter denied that he knew Jesus, or had anything to do with him. "At that moment … the Lord turned and looked at Peter …. and [Peter] went out and wept bitterly." Peter wept bitterly for his failure, for the person he was, and for his inability to change his attitude.

This leads us to look long and hard at the attitudes we hold towards our religion, towards our faith, towards the Church, towards our family and friends and neighbours, and towards ourselves. We need to be valued and cared for, loved and affirmed, but this cannot happen unless in return we value and esteem the people around us, and those closest to us. Our attitude is all-important, and we need constantly to bear it in mind. But this need not be a problem, to ourselves or to anyone else, if we keep before us the boundless and all-embracing love of God: "Let this mind be in you that was in Christ Jesus ..."

> *Father,*
> *give to us the mind*
> *that was in Christ Jesus,*
> *openness of heart to those around us,*
> *openness of spirit to know and do your will,*
> *so that our attitudes may be formed*
> *by our openness to your love,*
> *made known to us*
> *in your Son, Jesus Christ our Lord. Amen.*

Postcode lottery

"The NHS is a postcode lottery!" declare the news media. No doubt their criticism is justified. Hospitals vary enormously in their location, the buildings in which they are housed, their efficiency, and the standards of care which they offer. Obviously, this should not be so. Everyone, regardless of where they live, or who they are, should be able to receive the same high standards of care and treatment. But the provision remains uneven, and although there are reasons for this, it remains true that, even after sixty years of existence, the NHS is still seeking to provide an overall pattern of excellence.

The postcode lottery applies to other areas of life. The schools children attend vary enormously from one district to another. Most of our friends can expect an early-morning delivery of their mail. On an average day, ours arrives any time after noon. We find ourselves at the end of a long and tedious round for the postman. Some people choose where they will live according to the postcode. Geographically, we live closer to Blackheath, known in south-east London as a desirable residential area, but by postcode we belong to Lewisham, with its large immigrant population and rich ethnic and cultural mix. The difference in house prices between SE3 and SE13 – one digit in the postcode – can be several thousand pounds.

Life itself can be something of a postcode lottery. We are all the product of our birth, our early conditioning, our family circumstances, our education, or perhaps lack of it. We have known happiness and disappointment, joy and sadness, success and failure. We have all received God-given gifts which we may, or may not, have realised, may or may not have used, or been able to use. There is so much unpredictability in life, depending on who we are, what we are, and where we are at any given moment. I am acutely aware that if I had been born and brought up in some of the poorer parts of south-east London which form part of the background of my daily life, I would probably have turned out to be a very different person from the one that I now am. My thoughts and feelings would be different from what they are, and this book, in its present shape and form, would almost certainly never have been written.

This observation on my own background leads me to reflect further and more deeply on the historical context of my Christian faith. Let us suppose that Jesus had not been born in Bethlehem in the time of King Herod. Let us suppose instead that he had been born in our own time, an immigrant, in the enormous block of flats at the Elephant and Castle. Let us suppose further that he grew up to become a computer expert who could relate all the discoveries and opportunities of his technology to understanding the everyday needs of our human personalities. Would people have been open to his insights? Would his teaching have withstood the test of time, and developed into a worldwide movement? If so, what impact might it have had on the course of world events? What, we may wonder, would have been the end of this wonderful leader? Would he – or indeed, she – have met a violent death? Would there have been a belief that death was not the end for this special person, and that he or she rose from death and that his or her followers passionately believed in a continuing presence with them? Such speculation leads us to ponder again God's intervention in the core of human history. Why the place? Why the time? Was some sort of "postcode lottery" involved? Such questions lead us into deep theology, but they also lead us to think again about the place of God in our lives, and our calling as Christian people. Has our response to God come about through something of a "postcode lottery"? A welcoming church, a supportive friend, a chance remark, as in my own case, a local good cause which asked us to use our time and talents on their behalf? All these things, and many more, insignificant in themselves, can bring us to God.

In his first letter to the Church at Corinth, Paul reflects on how it has come about that it has fallen to him – he describes himself as "the least of the apostles" – to hand on the faith to his Christian brothers and sisters in that city. This great thinker and writer and Christian apologist seems unable to comprehend the magnitude of God's calling, and how it has come about. In the end, he can only acknowledge his perplexity, and hand it over to God: "By the grace of God, I am what I am." And so are we all. We reflect in later life on the way we have come, our path of faith, the way that has led us to God, and our awareness of his presence in our lives. We cannot account for the unexpected twists and turns in life, its glorious uncertainty, and its often scary unpredictability, by ascribing all that happens to fate, or chance or luck, either good or bad. Nor is it satisfactory, or personally satisfying, to think of life simply in terms of a "postcode lottery". We can only ponder the complexity of the deep ways of God. As the psalmist wrote:

"How weighty to me are your thoughts, O God!
How vast is the sum of them!
I try to count them – they are more than sand;
I come to the end – I am still with you."

> *Father, we rejoice*
> *that through your grace,*
> *we are what we are.*
> *Grant us now, in later years,*
> *to ponder the course of life,*
> *the way we have come,*
> *the way we are going,*
> *the meaning of life itself;*
> *and when we come to the end,*
> *to know we are still with you.*
> *Amen.*

Happy accidents

Words are our means of communication. We use them as our tools to carry our message, impart our news, convey our feelings. Some words seem to have a special quality. They feel good, like handling a piece of carved wood or polished stone. They have a gracious sound and carry an equally gracious meaning. "Serendipity" is just such a word. It was coined in the eighteenth century by the writer Horace Walpole from the old Persian fairy tale, *The Three Princes of Serendip*. Unfortunately, the word does not lend itself to being used in the course of everyday conversation, even though it describes something which probably happens to most of us, at least from time to time. It is the gift of being able to make delightful discoveries by pure accident.

At a reception for local clergy, I found myself talking to a priest whom I judged to be in his forties. We began to exchange who we were, where our ministry had taken us, and where we had originally come from. Before long, we discovered I had been at school with his mother, a pretty girl in the year below me, with curly blond hair, and bright blue eyes. All the boys were silently in love with her, myself included. Similarly, some years ago, when my wife and I were in Australia, a lady got off the bus at our stop. She was loaded with carrier bags, and I helped her down. "You're poms," she said, almost accusingly. "Where do you come from?" She was mollified when I told her we came from south-east London, and even more so when she discovered that our house was barely half a mile from where she had lived before she had emigrated many years before. Each one of us will have our own examples of making delightful discoveries by pure accident.

We find examples of serendipity in the New Testament. Fishermen Peter and Andrew, James and John, discovered one day as they were casting their nets in Lake Galilee, that they were being called to follow Jesus as his disciples. It was a delightful discovery, an opening to a new way of life. Similarly, a new way of life opened up for Matthew, "sitting at the tax booth". To be a tax collector for the loathed Roman authorities was to do a job which was hated and despised. With just a few words, he was changed from being a social outcast into a trusted disciple. The same was true of Zacchaeus, a chief tax-collector, who was so delighted to be accepted by Jesus, and called upon to be his host, that he promised to give half of his possessions to the poor, "and if I have defrauded anyone of anything, I will pay him back four times as much". This extravagant promise was an expression of the delight of his discovery. "The Son of Man came to seek out and to save the lost," responded Jesus. It was a moment of serendipity.

Later life can bring its moments of serendipity. It is a time when we may make delightful discoveries. Even if they are, to begin with, not entirely unintentional, it often happens that one discovery leads to another, so that our later discoveries do end up occurring by pure accident. Later life provides us with the opportunity to explore, to discover, to take up new areas of interest, to accomplish at last things we have been meaning to get round to for years. One of these might be our faith. It is easy to travel along the same religious tramlines, to carry with us unexpressed doubts, unvoiced questions. Now might well be the time to test out our ideas, to seek answers that we have long needed before it becomes too late. We have the opportunity to think the unthinkable, then wait to see what will happen. One thing we can be sure won't happen: God will not disappear. On the contrary, there may open up for us what we can recognise as great moments of serendipity – we make delightful discoveries by pure accident. And whatever we discover about God, about ourselves and about our faith, is a true blessing and a great delight.

Father,
we give thanks
for the moments in our lives
when we make discoveries
purely by accident,
about ourselves, about others,
about the meaning of life,
about the way we have come,
and about the way that lies ahead.
In our later years,
may we use the time you have given us
to discover more about you,
and find our delight
in the love you have made known to us
in your Son, Jesus Christ our Lord. Amen.

Defining moments

In July 2006, ceremonies were held to commemorate the seventieth anniversary of the beginning of the Spanish Civil War. It was the first major conflict between the forces of Fascism and Communism, and effectively formed the prelude to the outbreak of the Second World War in September 1939. That war in itself held many defining moments, not least the dropping of the first atomic bomb on Hiroshima in August 1945. Depending on our historical perspective, we can make our own list of what we consider to be the defining moments that have occurred during our lifetime: perhaps the first man in space, the assassination of John F. Kennedy, or the demolition of the Berlin Wall. There are many such moments to choose from, each with its own weight of significance.

Away from the sweep of history, there are defining moments in our own lives. They may not have appeared to be so at the time. They were insignificant in themselves, but materially affected and altered the course of our lives. I recall one such moment in the choir vestry after Evensong in the autumn of 1954. One of the senior choir members turned to me and said, "I hear you're thinking of taking holy orders." His casual remark came out of the blue. It caught me completely off guard, and shook me to the core. I had not long been demobilised at the end of my national service, and was wondering what I should do with my life, and where it was leading me. It had not occurred to me that it might be leading towards the ordained ministry, so I vigorously denied any thoughts or aspirations in that direction. As I did so, I recognised that I was not being true to myself. At that moment, I knew where my future lay. It was my first great defining moment.

A second was to follow soon after. I passed the Church of England's selection board, was recommended for ordination, and went for an interview at Salisbury Theological College, with a view to training there. The train home was packed. On the last part of the journey, an attractive young lady tumbled into the only vacant seat, which happened to be opposite to mine. I knew her slightly from attending church, where I admired her at a distance. The rest, as they say, is history, and my second great defining moment continues to define my life some fifty years later.

Many of us can look back over our lives and be aware of defining moments like these, but it is much more difficult to recognise new defining moments in later years. Yet they still happen. Decisions still have to be made about how we lead our lives now, and what provisions we make for the future. We may decide to take up new interests, or revive old ones that we have let slip. We may decide to rekindle old relationships, or enter into new ones. All these are defining moments, as may be the loss of those whom we have known and loved. Such moments may have a profound effect upon us. They tell us something, not only about the course of our lives, but about who we are, what we are, how we relate to one another, and ultimately, how we relate to God. As far as our faith is concerned, a defining factor may be the realisation that as we get older, we may move from an active and practical expression of our faith to one that is more reflective. It is a defining moment in parallel with the realisation that our physical energy and mental concentration and receptivity may not be at the same level of sharpness they once were.

If the defining moments of our later years are less heavily imprinted on our lives than those from when we were younger, there is some parallel between this and the Church's calendar over the course of the Christian year. All the major events – the defining moments – are concentrated into the first six months or so, from Advent to Trinity Sunday. There is very little to mark the course of events after that, and the Church's year seems to meander into quiet middle age, then into soporific old age as the Sundays after Trinity accumulate, and ordinary time drifts on. Then everything is rejuvenated on Advent Sunday: "Arise, shine; for your light has come" prophesies Isaiah.

The prophecy speaks to us, too, in our later years. It may have become a quieter time of life for us, but it will still have its moments of decision – defining moments in which God is active. Just as when we were younger, we need the light of God to guide us and direct us.

Heavenly Father,
be with us now in our later years.
Stir our hearts,
that we may be open to your love.
Open our minds
and give us understanding
of your direction and purpose in our lives.
Deepen our understanding,
to perceive and know your will for us.
In all the moments of decision
that confront us in our later years,
may we have faith to know
your presence is with us still
to shape and define the course of our lives.
We ask this for your name's sake. Amen.

Stereotypes

Some years ago, our younger daughter was admitted to hospital for emergency abdominal surgery. My wife and I visited her regularly and anxiously. After a day or two, the lady in the bed opposite caught my eye and beckoned me over. She made no mention of our daughter, what was the matter with her, or what progress she was making. She came straight to the point. "You're a vicar, aren't you," she said. "I've been watching you the last few days. I could tell."

How she could tell, I never found out, and I was too much taken aback to ask her. I asked myself what were the signs about me that she had read and interpreted so well; what were the messages that I had conveyed that I was, in her terms, "a vicar". As far as I was aware, I was a father very much concerned for his daughter, and visiting her in hospital as often as possible. Yet in some way, of which I was entirely unconscious, I must have been conforming to some kind of clerical stereotype. The lady in the bed opposite obviously spotted it, and, reasonably enough, felt that she needed her observations to be confirmed one way or the other.

The clerical stereotype has been with us for a long time. We can trace it from Chaucer, via Trollope, to *All Gas and Gaiters*, *Dad's Army*, *Father Ted* and *The Vicar of Dibley*. From a positive point of view, stereotypes help to remind us of how the rest of the world sees us. They encourage us to laugh at ourselves, not to take ourselves too seriously. They help to keep us earthed in reality, and in touch with the life of the world around us. They remind us that the things which are important to us may be of little consequence to other people. In this way, stereotypes can be stimulating and liberating.

Yet sometimes they can have the opposite effect. The line between stereotype and caricature is a thin one. The former is defined as a rigidly conventional expression of an idea or character. Caricature is ridicule by exaggeration or distortion, often with a mocking or offensive intention. We find people difficult when they behave as their stereotype would suggest. They prevent any real communication, or the genuine expression and exchange of thoughts and ideas. It is surely not intentional on their part, but we find that we are prevented from coming anywhere near them as real people. Not only is this difficult for us, we find it frustrating and irritating. So we counter it with caricature, unworthy as it may be, and seek our revenge in that way. But then I also have to admit that we deal with people in this rather harsh way, not only because we find them irritating, but because, more importantly, by being what they are, they pose some kind of threat to us and our sense of well-being.

We see this in the caricatures of the third age. Take, for example, the warning triangle in the Highway Code to alert drivers to the possibility of elderly people crossing the road. A bent man and a stooping woman, leaning heavily on their sticks, totter unsteadily across the road, presenting as much real danger to themselves as to anyone else. I wonder whether that is stereotype, caricature, or just plain exaggeration. It is little surprise, therefore, to read that we are referred to as "wrinklies" or "crumblies". These demeaning words would scarcely be allowed in other contexts. In a world which is increasingly geared to sport, the pursuits of young people, and the expression of physical prowess, no one wants to be reminded that the years when all this is possible pass all too quickly. We ourselves were that age once – though younger people may find that hard to believe – and they too will be as we are now, in the not-too-distant future. We represent an inevitable and unwelcome reminder of the passage of time, and the transitory nature of life itself. This was brought home to the disciples when the risen Jesus said to Peter:

"Very truly, I tell you, when you were younger, you used to fasten your own belt and go wherever you wished. But when you grow old, you will stretch out your hands, and someone else will fasten a belt around you and take you where you do not wish to go." Perhaps some of us have reached that point, either literally or metaphorically, already. For some of us, it may happen eventually. For others, it may never happen at all. We simply do not know, nor can we tell. For the moment, life is ours to live, appreciate and enjoy, as fully and as freely as we can. On that account, we may reassure those who come after us. We pose no threat to them, nor do we wish to do so. There is no need for them to protect themselves by casting stereotype and caricature upon us. We are all part of the continuing life and unfolding pattern of God's creation.

Lord God, our Creator,
you have made us all in your image
to bear the reflection of your glory.
Forgive us, we pray,
when we seek to diminish others
by casting upon them
the limitations of our own image.
May we accept them
as we pray they will accept us
in the name of Jesus our Saviour,
who by his dying and rising
offers acceptance to us all. Amen.

Gentleness

Gentle Jesus, meek and mild,
Look upon a little child.
Pity my simplicity,
Suffer me to come to thee.

One of my early childhood memories is of my mother kneeling by
the side of my bed, saying that old prayer either to me or for me –
probably a bit of both. I didn't understand it, or what it was all
about, but it felt good, and was a comforting part of my going-to-
bed routine. The impression it made was reinforced as I grew up,
by the well-known picture of Jesus, with long, flowing, golden hair,
and a well-trimmed blond beard, surrounded by children of
various nationalities and all colours. It was a picture that found its
way into many schoolrooms, and was a sentimental illustration of
Jesus' words recorded in Mark 10:14: "Suffer the little children to
come unto me." The verse, as I recall, was the title of the painting,
and presented Jesus, as he has scornfully been called, as "the pale
Galilean".

The image was one which I, and no doubt many like me, found
difficult to unlearn, and it remained with me as I grew up. But that
childhood image could not have been farther from the truth. Jesus
must have been an extremely robust character. Tough is a word
that comes to mind. On a physical level, he led a nomadic
existence, travelling from place to place with his disciples – "The
son of Man has nowhere to lay his head." On a personal level, he
confronted and denounced the entrenched customs and traditions
of the Jewish establishment, knowing, no doubt, what this would
ultimately lead to: "The Son of Man is going to be betrayed into
human hands, and they will kill him." So, at times, his teaching
could be equally stern for his disciples: "Do not think that I have

come to bring peace to the earth ... but a sword ...Those who find their life will lose it, and those who lose their life for my sake will find it."

All this is far removed from "gentle Jesus, meek and mild". Yet one of the most appealing and enduring images of Jesus is that of the Good Shepherd. It presents us with a pastoral simplicity which reaches out to us and touches us. Not only that, the image of the Good Shepherd is deeply rooted in Jewish culture and tradition, recurring many times in the Old Testament. "The Lord is my shepherd, therefore I shall not want," wrote the psalmist. So we are presented with a balance in the ministry, preaching and teaching of Jesus: a balance between robustness and gentleness, between activity and quietness, between challenge and affirmation. This balance provides, and has always provided, the traditional pattern of Christian pastoral ministry. The two elements of robustness and gentleness are necessary, not only for those who exercise a pastoral ministry, but for all of us as Christian people, as we seek to maintain a healthy balance which both deepens our faith, and enriches every aspect of our lives.

So I try to keep this balance in the way my life works out day by day. Nevertheless, there are days when I feel less than robust, either physically, emotionally, or spiritually. I recognise that this is all part of the ageing process. So on days like these, my need is for gentleness. I do not want to be faced with a challenge, a word I find still popular with preachers, and which I hear in many sermons. Rather, I am happy to hear the call of the Good Shepherd, and to follow where he leads. I know I am going to be fed, like the sheep in the field next to the vicarage in my brief years as a country vicar. In winter, Jim, the farmer, would come with bundles of hay, calling to the sheep as he approached the field. They came running to his call. No doubt he knew them, and could recognise them all. So the Good Shepherd knows us, his flock. He calls us by name.

We respond to this. It is the pattern of a close relationship based on trust, expectation, hope and fulfilment. All these are qualities which are precious to us at any stage of life, but especially so in later life when they are heightened by our increasing years.

St Paul, as an apostle, was another robust character, but he too was aware of the importance of gentleness as a means of building up his Christian converts in the faith. "We were gentle among you," he wrote to the Church in Thessalonica, looking back over his ministry there, presumably among the old as well as the young. In his letter to the Galatians, he includes gentleness as one of the gifts of the Spirit. "Be gentle to everyone," is the advice given in the letter to Titus. Those of us in later life may want to explore those words further in order to reach a fuller and deeper understanding of the gentleness of God.

> *Lord Jesus, Good Shepherd,*
> *who laid down your life for your sheep so that you*
> *   might take it again,*
> *and be with us for ever;*
> *deal gently with us, we pray, especially in our*
> *   later years.*
> *May we know your voice,*
> *obey your call,*
> *and follow where you lead,*
> *so that we may be one flock*
> *with you, our one shepherd,*
> *now, and in the life to come. Amen.*

A sense of humour

In the spring of 2002, Peter Price, suffragan Bishop of Kingston, left the Diocese of Southwark to become Bishop of Bath and Wells. He bade farewell to the diocese where, he said, he had spent twenty happy years, with these words of encouragement: "My prayer ... is that you may eat, drink, laugh, watch bad movies, listen to jazz, and work at building the interconnected covenantal relationships which make up the kingdom of God."

With this apparently light touch, Bishop Peter managed to convey in his message the essence of the Christian faith. Of course we must work hard as we strive to establish the kingdom of God in a visible and recognisable form here on earth. But we must not do so in a way which prevents other people as well as ourselves from enjoying all the good gifts of life which God has created, and presented to us to enjoy. Jesus himself had time to enjoy meals and fellowship with his friends and disciples. We must never allow the practice of our faith to become a religious straitjacket and so miss out on the fun and humour that are an essential part of it. In later life, I reflect with sadness on how often those qualities seem to be missing, and how easy it is to become hooked-in to one particular outlook, chained to one selective interpretation or point of view. One aspect of the faith can become so magnified, and receive such emphasis, that any other approach may seem to be insubstantial, lacking something essential, or just plain wrong. Small details in the way we do things take on major proportions, and just as easily become stumbling blocks to others. It is important to be able to see how readily we organise ourselves into rigid institutions and fail to be aware of the ridiculous in the structures of the institutional Church. If only we have the humility to laugh at ourselves, at our foibles and our failings, we can perhaps recognise the smallness of our horizons which impedes our spiritual growth, and stunts our maturity as Christian people. A sense of the absurd ensures that we maintain a healthy balance in life, and keep things in perspective. This is something we need in order to function effectively as people, and to practise a balanced religious faith. So much of what we invest in the outward forms of religion has little to say about the love of God, or the coming of God's kingdom.

This may be something of which we become more conscious in later life, when we can disentangle ourselves from the immediate situation, and have the space and time to stand aside and see things more clearly for what they are. This can be difficult when we are still immersed in our daily work. I found that there were times during my ministry when my sense of humour ceased to work, and my sense of proportion suffered accordingly. I knew then that was time for a holiday which would take me at least a hundred miles away. Geographical distance was important. However, if my sense of humour still failed to work when I returned, then it was time to start thinking about a move to a fresh sphere of work. Without a sense of humour, we are inflicting a heavy burden on ourselves, on those close to us, on our Church, and ultimately on our faith.

Perhaps there were times when Jesus felt himself to be weighed down with a similar sort of burden. Luke records how Jesus became entangled in a dispute with the scribes and Pharisees on a technical point about receiving baptism from John the Baptist. Nothing was right for them. They had lost all sense of proportion. Jesus said that they were "like children sitting in the market-place and calling to one another, 'We played the flute for you, and you did not dance; we wailed, and you did not weep.'" It was a wry comment on an exasperating situation. Jesus evidently hoped that by using this fairly humorous comparison, he might persuade his opponents to see how entrenched they were in the traditions of their religious faith.

Perhaps a sense of humour will help us to remain aware of how entrenched we can become with the passage of time. Our later years are marked with the foibles of our personal traditions. We do the same things, in the same way, at the same times. We find it easier that way, rather than to break out of established routines. I have to confess to being very fond of what I like to call "my automatic pilot". But if my sense of humour is working, I can manage to acknowledge that it would probably be better to do something differently, or even try something different, just for its own sake. We certainly need a sense of humour to help us cope with the ageing process as a whole, and to be able to laugh, or at least smile, at ourselves in recognising what we are no longer able to do. This is, I believe, a great blessing. And if it is a blessing, then it comes from God who also, I like to believe, has a sense of humour. Otherwise God would have given up on me a long time ago. Even now, in my later years, God seems able to puncture my self-centredness and self-importance when they threaten to get out of hand. When this happens, I have a wry smile to myself – and perhaps God has a chuckle as well.

In spite of – or perhaps because of – the troubles and tribulations they have been through, the Jewish people have never lost their ability to laugh at themselves. So to end, here is a very Jewish joke, sent to me by my oldest friend, who is herself Jewish, and lives in Jerusalem: "An ultra-orthodox rabbi died and went to heaven. When he arrived, he was offered a meal to refresh him after his journey. 'Tell me,' he said, 'who is in charge of the kosher arrangements here?' 'The Almighty himself,' was the reassuring answer. 'Thanks,' said the rabbi, 'I'll just have a glass of water.'"

Heavenly Father,
you know us better than we know ourselves,
and are aware of every aspect of our being.
With all your other gifts,
grant to us a sense of humour,
so that we may laugh at ourselves,
and keep in proportion the demands
with which we surround our faith.
So may we be open to you,
and know at the centre of our lives
the love revealed to us in your Son,
Jesus Christ our Lord. Amen.

Decisions, decisions!

Angela Huth's novel *Land Girls* tells the story of three young women from different walks of life who joined the Women's Land Army in the early days of the 1939-45 war. Prue was the most "forward" (to use an old expression) of the three. She had a brief, but passionate, affair with the farmer's son. Then, within a short time of meeting him at a dance in the local town hall, she married a good-looking young airman serving with Bomber Command. Tragically, soon after their marriage, he failed to return from a bombing raid. His aircraft had been hit by enemy fire, and crashed down into the sea. Prue is devastated by the news, and as Ag and Stella, the other two land girls, try to calm and comfort her, she screams hysterically at them that if they have the chance to meet and marry the man they want, they should not hesitate. They must seize the moment, take the opportunity while it is there; it may never present itself again.

The story has many twists and turns, but in many ways these words of Prue form the pivotal moment. Ag follows Prue's advice. When she meets her man, she hangs on to him. He survives the war, and they live "happily ever after". Stella follows her conscience rather than her heart. She makes a decision which she knows is not well founded, and intrinsically wrong. She marries the wrong man for what she tells herself are the best of reasons. She has to live with the pain of the subsequent break-up of her marriage when her husband leaves her for another woman. The man she wanted to marry was the farmer's son, who loved her dearly in return. He was left bereft and bewildered at Stella's apparent change of heart. Prue's words, and the advice which she had screamed from the depths of her tragedy, came back to haunt Stella over the years. She had recognised the critical moment in her life, the decision that had to be made – and she had turned away.

Critical moments, critical questions and critical decisions are by no means confined to people in the prime of life, even questions to do with meeting the "right" person and forming a satisfactory and harmonious relationship. There are those of us who know the deep feeling of well-being from finding and experiencing love, long-lasting affection and companionship, in our later years. The decision as to whether we should make that commitment with all its various implications is a far-reaching one. Other decisions which face us in later life are no less significant. There are issues to be decided in the area of finance, especially with regard to pension provision, and a will to be drawn and kept updated. There are decisions to be faced regarding dependence and independence. We have to decide at some stage if and when we should move, whether or not we should "downsize", when and how to dispose of belongings that have formed part of our daily life and background for many years. All these questions, the answers we make, and the decisions we reach, are critical. They are turning points (which is essentially the meaning of the word crisis). We have to go one way or another. There is no middle ground, and no turning back. Of course, we have met such moments all through our lives, and we are not strangers to them. But perhaps we had more energy – emotional as well as physical – to bring to bear in our younger years than we do now. Also, we had the reassurance of knowing that if we had made a mistake or an unwise decision, we still had time to redeem the situation, or try an alternative. That option is less open to us at our stage of life. We may look back with some degree of wistfulness to the time when it seemed so much easier to take things in our stride.

However, I do sometimes wonder if this really was so, and whether we ever reached major decisions in life with complete certainty, and without some degree of hesitation. This applies to our faith. There are many Christians who can recall with accuracy the place and the moment when they decided to respond to God's call, and to dedicate their lives to Christ. There are many others who are not conscious of any such moment of decision, but who rejoice to find themselves numbered among the servants of God. We find examples of both kinds of response in the Bible. Moses, Isaiah and Jeremiah all hesitated to respond to God's call because of a deep feeling of unworthiness. Faced with the personal summons of Jesus, the closest disciples followed him without delay. Around the fringes there was less certainty. Yet Jesus was adamant: "No one who puts a hand to the plough and looks back is fit for the Kingdom of God." And for himself: "When the days drew near for him to be taken up, he set his face to go to Jerusalem." There was no turning back. The decision had been made.

On one level, this is a daunting prospect, especially as we know what lay ahead for Jesus. Certainly he did, too. On another level, it can be a source of strength and encouragement. Often there is a feeling of intrinsic "rightness" in the conclusions we come to, and the decisions we make. This "rightness", I like to believe, is God-given – part of the movement of the Spirit in our lives. Sometimes the decisions are less clear-cut, and become an act of faith.

"Seize the moment," screamed Prue in the depths of her distress ... "Make the most of the opportunity." In spite of our doubts and hesitation, when we make our decision in good faith, we can rest assured that it is acceptable to God.

Loving Father,
look gently upon us
in the perplexities which confront us,
in the decisions we must make.
By your Spirit, grant us
humility to lay our doubts before you,
wisdom to perceive what is right,
courage to face what is unclear,
strength of purpose to move ahead,
and openness of heart and mind
to know your presence with us. Amen.

The child within

The year 2006 marked the two-hundredth anniversary of the birth of the great engineer, Isambard Kingdom Brunel. He is arguably best remembered for his construction of the Great Western Railway, and its London terminus at Paddington station. One of his early projects was a joint venture with his father, the building of the Rotherhithe tunnel in south-east London, the first tunnel under the river Thames. It nearly cost the young Brunel his life when the roof collapsed, and the water poured in. I walked through the tunnel late one night after the electric current for the underground trains had been switched off. It was still possible to see from the original brickwork just how painstakingly the tunnel had been dug out. I have made other such pilgrimages, to the National Railway Museum at York, with its magnificent collection of old locomotives and rolling stock, and to the great red-brick frontage of St Pancras station, which, until now, has stood largely unused since the original hotel closed in the early 1930s.

Like many clergy I have a passion for steam trains. It is not surprising, therefore, that I should choose to spend my seventieth birthday on a visit to one of the preserved lines and a trip on a steam-hauled train. Nothing can beat the sight and smell of an engine in live steam, and this was a monster! I felt that this was a day when I could justifiably acknowledge, and even indulge, the child within.

More often, my attention is caught by the aircraft which fly in over our house in south-east London on their way in to land at Heathrow, some twenty miles to the west. Concorde always gave me a great thrill. Despite all the many evenings I had seen it, I always made a point of watching its sleek elegance when I heard the roar of its great engines approaching. The crowning moment was Concorde's final day, when three of them flew in, just ninety seconds apart. It was a moment not to be missed, and never repeated. Whether it's trains, planes, or a variety of other things, the child within me is alive and well.

One of the regrets of life must surely be that the naturalness of childhood is suppressed so early and then gradually eroded. Realistically, it has to be so, but there is a corresponding loss of spontaneity that inevitably deprives our personality of some of its essential vitality. The episode of my mother taking the four-year-old me out to tea at the home of a well-to-do friend became a family joke, often retold. "Mummy," I complained, "this cake's stale." It was – but I had to learn that you can't say things like that, you have to learn to be polite. From this point on, I was embarked on the process of recognising awkward situations, not asking difficult questions, and not passing comments on people's dress and behaviour. We learn the process of passing our natural responses through a series of filters before they are put into words. We are conditioned to behave in ways that are socially acceptable, and we are judged socially on the degree of acceptability that we manage to attain. All of that is necessary if we are to function as social beings in life as we know it, but the price we pay can be heavy. In the process, we may lose the directness, openness, enthusiasm and spontaneity of our early years. Those early qualities cannot be recaptured. We recall the words of St Paul: "When I was a child, I spoke like a child, I thought like a child, I reasoned like a child; when I became an adult, I put an end to childish ways." If we think that we can consciously and deliberately recreate them in our later years, we deceive ourselves. For being what we think is open and outspoken, we can be labelled grumpy old men or women.

So now, well established in my third age, I find great satisfaction in taking the opportunity to re-create and to re-live the pleasures of my childhood and teens. All being well, that is something which is open to us all. I make sandcastles on the beach when we are on holiday with our grandchildren, and if they wander off and choose to do something else, I am happy to carry on without them. When I go to the pantomime, I boo and hiss and shout "It's behind you!" in all the right places without any inhibitions at all. In her contribution to *Spirituality and Ageing* (ed. Albert Jewell, published by Jessica Kingsley 1999), Helen Oppenheimer writes: "When people have to retire because they are too old to work, must they be stuck in idleness, which has no point and is bound to pall? The opposite of work need not be uselessness, or even rest, it might be play …Work has to have a point or it is soul-destroying, but play is its own point." She speaks for the child within us all in a way which I find extremely affirming. It is a profound observation which she makes, which reflects the words of Jesus: "Truly I tell you, whoever does not receive the kingdom of God as a little child will never enter it." As we make contact again in our later life with the child within us, we rediscover and explore the kingdom once more.

> *Heavenly Father,*
> *we remember the words of your Son,*
> *that unless we become as children,*
> *we should not enter his kingdom.*
> *Preserve within us, we pray,*
> *the openness of heart and mind*
> *that we see in our children,*
> *the willingness to learn,*
> *the desire to explore,*
> *and the spontaneity to respond*
> *with interest to all things new,*
> *so that with heart and mind*
> *we may use these gifts*
> *to enrich our lives*
> *and deepen our faith*
> *in the service of your kingdom,*
> *and of your Son, Jesus Christ our Lord. Amen.*

A new member of the family

Our first grandchild was small when she was born. I remember cradling her head in my hand, and supporting her tiny body along my forearm, her feet tucked in the crook of my elbow. I marvelled then at the whole act of creation which she represented. "The divine activity, the life of the whole cosmos across the ages," I wrote at the time, "seemed to be gathered up and expressed through the birth of this child." Thirteen years later, our third grandchild was born, also a girl. I was no less thankful for her safe arrival, or for the wonder of creation which she represented. This new baby, formed and grown within my other daughter, had now made her appearance, a new little person, a new member of our family and of the human family as a whole.

But what also struck me was the sweep of time, probably because I am now that much older. I was in my early sixties when our first grandchild was born. Now I am in my mid-seventies. As I thought about it, I realised that I represent a midpoint in something like two hundred or more years of family history. My grandparents were born in the 1870s. This new grandchild, all being well, should live to see the 2070s, and perhaps even beyond that, if she has inherited the genes of longevity on my wife's side of the family.

I find this span of years both fascinating, and yet difficult to assimilate. My grandchildren could be telling their grandchildren about what their grandparents told them about their grandparents. Yet this degree of continuity is with us all the time. It is nowhere better to be seen than in the life of the Church. "Lord thou hast been our refuge, from one generation to another," writes the psalmist. We are successors to those who in their own generation have received the Christian faith, entered into it, and interpreted it. Key to the issue is the fundamental Christian belief that at a certain moment in time, the infinite God made himself known, and entered the finite world which he had created, in the person of his Son, Jesus Christ. The Gospels tell us something of what happened, and the epistles give us some clue as to the results of what happened, and the meaning that the first Christians attached to it. But it is this critical meeting of time and eternity, the finite and infinite, that constitutes the foundation point of our Christian faith, the faith that has gathered up succeeding generations ever since.

Each generation has sought to relate the faith to the needs of contemporary society, and restate it according to its demands. Thus the early Church had to deal with the questions posed by its Jewish roots. The medieval Church had to face the prevalence of superstition and the belief in magic within society as a whole, and among its own people. The Renaissance Church was challenged by the scientific discoveries. The nineteenth-century Church had to respond to the onset of the Industrial Revolution, and all the problems it brought in its wake. The twentieth century was scarred by two great world wars, and the disillusionment and indifference to organised religion which came about as a result. Perhaps no one caught the mood better than the Revd Geoffrey Studdert-Kennedy. As an army chaplain, affectionately known as "Woodbine Willie", he had witnessed and shared the horror of the trenches during the First World War, and afterwards knew only too well that the servicemen who had survived were not returning to the "land fit for heroes" they had been promised by the government of the day. He also felt keenly that the church was not doing as much as he had hoped and anticipated in order to alleviate the situation. So his memorable poem "Indifference", written in protest, imagines a contemporary scene:

When Jesus came to Birmingham they simply passed him by,
They never hurt a hair of him, they only let him die;
For men had grown more tender, and they would not give him
pain,
They only just passed down the street, and left him in the rain.

A mainly kindly, tolerant, bemused indifference continues into the twenty-first century. The Church of our own day has to find the means of responding to a time of perhaps unprecedented affluence, unlimited choice, the impact of technology, and a way of life based upon it and dependent on it. In every age it has been, and still is, the task of the Church to relate a message which has its roots in the rural life of Palestine two thousand years ago, to the needs, outlook and demands of contemporary society.

Paradoxically, it is these problems and challenges to the faith which unify succeeding generations of Christian people. As I suggested earlier, I can see myself as the connecting point for two hundred years of history in my own family. When we look at the family of God, we can see connections which take us back much further in time, and, under God, into the future as well. We rejoice to be part of that family, and as with our own families, to do whatever we can to build up its wellbeing with life-enhancing relationships. In doing so, we respond to what St Paul referred to as "the heavenly call of God in Christ Jesus". We have sought to build upon what has been handed on to us from previous generations, so that we in turn may hand on our Christian heritage to generations still to come.

God, the Father of all infinity,
we know that all our time
is in your hands.
We give thanks for the succeeding generations,
within our families,
and within your Church,
and for the common faith
that binds us together.
Guide us, we pray,
as we seek to relate our faith
to the world in which we live,
and as you have guided and inspired
those who have gone before us,
so be with those
who will come after us,
in the name of Jesus Christ, our Lord. Amen.

New freedom

Later life can bring us a wide range of financial concessions. We may be able to get senior citizens' rates for the cinema, theatre, bus and rail travel. Some hotels offer bargain breaks for older people at less busy times of the year. The most generous concession for those of us who live in London is the "Freedom Pass". This allows almost unlimited free off-peak travel on buses, trains and the underground, right across the capital and even beyond in some directions. Even though the Freedom Pass is funded by means of the Council Tax, it represents a significant rebate, worth more each year as fares inevitably rise. Obviously, it is not without its political overtones – the "grey vote" is important to all the political parties – but seen at its best, the freedom pass aims to live up to its title, by keeping older people mobile and active, providing them with the motivation to remain socially aware and to know what is going on, and to be able to participate should they so wish. Some older people enjoy using their Freedom Pass for its own sake, and from time to time I come across people who are taking the opportunity to explore the capital for the first time. It is something that they have always intended to do, and now, with their Freedom Pass, they are able to do it. London lies open to them – which is freedom indeed!

It is good to be able to do something like this, something we do simply because we want to do it. That is reason enough in itself, free of any feeling of obligation to anyone except ourselves. This kind of freedom can be quite difficult to achieve. Many of us have spent a lifetime, whether at home or at work, feeling that we are under a sense of obligation to family, relatives, friends, employers, and to our fellow-workers. We may need to take a major step of inner persuasion, and offload a pervading, residual sense of guilt, to be able to choose what we want to do, and to do it when we choose.

This is one area we can explore in later life, even though it can be quite scary moving beyond the familiar marker-buoys, and moving out onto an uncharted sea. This is something I find easier to write about than to put into practice. My personality is such that (changing my metaphor, because I am the world's worst sailor) I prefer to stick to my usual tramlines. I know which routes lead where, and where the stopping places are. But even with all my reservations and hesitation, I can recognise that it would be wrong to allow myself to be tied down in this way. When I do set off from time to time, not knowing exactly where I am heading for, I find that I enjoy the freedom of exploring. I feel that I have really achieved something by discovering new places, learning something about them, and meeting new people.

However, all this is outward exploration. In later life, we are free to make inward exploration as well, of ourselves, and of our faith. "If you continue in my word," said Jesus, "you are truly my disciples; and you will know the truth, and the truth will make you free." This freedom is well illustrated by a verse from St Paul which I have always regarded as pivotal in my understanding of the Christian faith, and in my call to the ministry. Chapter thirteen of 1 Corinthians claims so much of our attention, and is so well-known, that we completely overlook the previous chapter. But that is where my inspiration lies: "There are varieties of gifts," writes Paul, "but the same spirit." I first came across this verse as a student, when I was caught up with a group of Christians who were making me feel very inadequate. They seemed to know all the answers at a time when I could barely begin to frame the questions. When I discovered Paul's words, I experienced an enormous sense of freedom. I suddenly realised that it was all right to be me. I did not have to be like the other young men in the group, or conform to what even then I felt was a very restricted outlook on the Christian faith. I had my own gifts, my own value, my own worth, and I believed that God was calling me to use them on his behalf in the ordained ministry of the Church.

As I revisit the words from 1 Corinthians 12 in later life, I realise that I have to explore them further to find what meaning they hold for me now. By the nature of things, I was able to use only a limited number of my gifts during my years of ministry. Some of them I still use, but there are others which have been neglected or set aside for a long period of time. They need to be rediscovered, put back into use again, and enjoyed. For some of us, these gifts will show themselves in new interests, new directions, a new and satisfying diversity in life. Others will take us inwards, enable us to explore our faith, and deepen our belief in God. The freedom which is ours in later life can enrich our final years and bring us closer to God, the author and giver of all good gifts.

Father, we thank you
for the diverse gifts of your Spirit
which we have used in your service
in our lives until now.
In our later years,
bring us to a new understanding
of how many gifts within us
remain to be revealed.
May we use our freedom
to explore them and enjoy them,
and find in them a sense of fulfilment
which will deepen our love for you,
and for your Son, Jesus Christ our Lord. Amen.

In the middle of the night

"How did you sleep?" I find myself asking my wife most mornings, a routine opening to the day, knowing that I slept well, and enjoyed my usual seven or even eight hours of unbroken slumber.

But there are nights when I do not sleep quite so soundly. I may have drunk too much before going to bed, or eaten too heavily, so that my digestive system is still hard at work. More often I have something on my mind, something that I am working on, something that refuses to go away, and that I cannot easily resolve. Other times there seems to be no apparent reason for not sleeping well, or at worst, not sleeping at all. Sometimes I wake in the small hours, and know beyond any shadow of doubt that I am not going to be able to get back to sleep again. Many of us will have had the same experience. We try lying this way and that. We toss and we turn. In the end, whatever the clock may say, and however much our internal bodyclock may protest, there is nothing for it but to get up, and, for myself, make a cup of tea.

The small hours can be a dreadful time to be awake. I discovered during the nights I spent on guard duty during my national service, that 2.00am to 4.00am is the deepest and loneliest part of the night. It was the shift we all tried to avoid. I discovered years later as a chaplain at Guy's hospital in London, that those are the only two hours when the capital comes anywhere near to sleeping. When we find we can't sleep, we can feel very much alone and extremely vulnerable. My cup of tea helps. The all-night TV provides some kind of virtual company, and if we wish to hear a human voice speaking live, BBC World Service takes over when Radio Four comes to an end.

Yet it is also possible to be positive about our night-time wakefulness. We may know, for instance, that we do not have to be up to go to work in the morning, and that we can probably allow ourselves a nap in the middle of the day. We also know from our experience that whatever was keeping us awake will look less worrying, and assume more manageable proportions, by the light of day. We know, if we think about it, that many people are working through the night, or up and about for various reasons, as we are ourselves. So ultimately we are not alone, and what is happening to us is a shared experience. We can also put our period of wakefulness during the small hours to good use.

We may choose to reflect on our inner store of experience. We may reflect on the way we have come, where we are now, and whatever lies ahead. We have concerns for the present and hopes for the future, both for ourselves, and those whom we hold near and dear. This may lead us into prayer, and we may find ourselves reflecting on our religious faith and outlook. There is nothing outwardly to disturb us, so maybe we can become aware of God's presence in the deep silence which surrounds us, even become aware of that "still, small voice" which is usually so elusive. The middle of the night can be an opportunity to be with God, something that may not happen all that often. We are told that Jesus "withdrew ... to a deserted place by himself," and, on another occasion, encouraged the disciples to do the same. In the middle of the night, we may be aware of the presence of Jesus with us. Instead of feeling alone and isolated in the silence of the small hours, we shall feel strengthened, comforted, enriched.

Eventually the dawn breaks, and gradually the daylight establishes itself once more. Life begins to stir, and we can begin to face another day, feeling more positive than seemed possible a few hours earlier. We pick up the threads of our daily routine – and hope that we sleep better tonight.

Father of all time,
be with us in the small hours of the night,
when sleep eludes us,
all is silent, nothing stirs,
and the tide of life
seems at its lowest ebb.
May we use the time
to open ourselves to your love,
to lay before you our memories,
our innermost thoughts, our fears,
our concerns for those whom we know and love,
our hopes for the future,
and our regrets for the past.
In the silence,
speak to us in your still, small voice,
so we may find confidence in your presence
to support us in the day ahead,
so that we may serve you, and one another,
for your sake. Amen.

Night as bright as the day

Stonehenge remains one of the mysteries of the English landscape. Archaeologists know how it was built, and where the building materials came from, but what it was built for, no one really knows. It is significant that on midsummer's day, the rays of the rising sun shine directly onto what seems to have been some kind of altar, perhaps where ritual sacrifices took place, but there is no means of knowing. One can only speculate.

However we do know for certain that, along with other natural objects such as trees and running water, our ancestors worshipped the moon and the sun. "You have made the moon to mark the seasons," wrote the psalmist; "the sun to rule over the day, the moon and the stars to rule over the night". Whatever the official religion of those Old Testament times, it was still necessary to keep on the right side of nature. It still is. As well as the whole impetus of the ecological movement, many newspapers and magazines publish horoscopes purporting to tell of the influence of the stars upon our lives, and, over recent years, many of us have become sun-worshippers too; a flight of two hours can whisk us away a thousand miles to enjoy sunshine and increased levels of daylight, especially during the long dark days of the British winter.

The contrast between darkness and light is deeply embedded in the imagery of the Bible, representing the struggle between good and evil. In the Genesis story, the first thing that God created was light: "God saw that the light was good; and God separated the light from the darkness." John develops this theme in the Prologue of his Gospel: "The life was the light of all people. The light shines in the darkness, and the darkness did not overcome it." Jesus fulfils those words in his own person: "I am the light of the world. Whoever follows me will never walk in darkness, but will know the light of life."

The liturgy between Advent and Candlemas (the presentation of Our Lord) is full of this imagery. In the words of St Paul, "let us lay aside the works of darkness and put on the armour of light". When Mary and Joseph brought the infant Jesus to present him in the Temple, "Simeon took him in his arms and praised God," calling the child "a light for revelation to the Gentiles, and for glory to your people Israel". Christmas itself is celebrated in a blaze of light, a reminder that the Christian festival was superimposed on the old pagan celebration of the midwinter solstice, and the return of the light after its autumnal dying. It is perhaps arguable that the number of lights on display at Christmas increases in proportion as fewer people subscribe to the traditional Christmas story, and celebrate instead what has been called the "winterval". However that may be, Christians believe they have a high calling to "live as children of light – for the fruit of the light is to be found in all that is good and right and true". "We are children of the day," writes St Paul, "We are not of the night or of darkness." The meaning of the imagery of darkness and light could not be more clearly stated.

However, I sometimes wonder whether there is too much light in our world. I recognise that this is contradictory, especially bearing in mind one particularly stressful journey on an unlit motorway, in pouring rain, and traffic nose-to-tail all the way. How glad I was to see the lights of London in the distance. Yet I know that the light generated by great cities may be causing considerable harm. Europe, viewed by a satellite high above the Earth, is one blaze of light, and the brightest part is centred on the UK. Ecologists tell us that constant light is interfering with the natural rhythms of our world. Just locally, in the trees around our house, birds are still singing well into the late evening, when, in the natural order of things, they would be roosting. Our urban foxes are no longer nocturnal animals. There is so much light at night – and so much food available at all times – that they seem indifferent as to what time of day or night they choose to appear. So instead of praying, "Lighten our darkness" (as found in the evening prayer of the Anglican Church) we should perhaps be asking, "Darken our lightness."

This apparently facetious observation in fact makes good sense and equally good theology. God did not banish darkness in the Genesis story, but merely separated it from the light. "God called the light Day, and the darkness he called Night." We need to rehabilitate the concept of darkness. Instead of regarding it as negative, the opposite of all that is good and wholesome and life-giving, we need to see darkness as being positive in itself. According to the Genesis story once again, it is the medium through which the world came into being: "darkness covered the face of the deep". It is the medium, too, through which we ourselves have life and being. The sperm fertilises the egg in the darkness of the womb, where we are conceived and develop in safety. It is only when we are born that we emerge into the light of day.

At the other end of life, we reflect on the periods of light and darkness in our lives, the periods of growth, and the periods of stagnation, the times of success, and the times of failure, the times of happiness, and the times of sadness, the times of personal fulfilment, and the times of debilitation. Experience tells us that life is full of opposites, and that to live life to the full, we have to hold the opposites in balance. Once again, the psalmist expresses these thoughts for us: "Even the darkness is not dark to you; the night is as bright as the day, for darkness is as light to you."

Father Creator,
we give thanks
for the darkness of our creation,
for the light that has sustained us,
and still guides our lives.
May we know your presence
in both darkness and light
and grow daily in the image
of your Son, Jesus Christ our Lord. Amen.

Friends

My wife and I are fortunate in having a wide circle of friends. We are perhaps rather less fortunate in that they are so far apart geographically. We have made our friends as we have moved around, living and working in Yorkshire, Lancashire, Cambridge and London. We also have friends and family in our native Midlands. Christmas cards are a means by which we keep in touch once a year. We write a brief message of news and greeting, and express the good intention of really trying to meet up again. In practice, we find that, as we get older, it can take more effort and motivation to bring that about than it used to. Added to which, because of distance, there may realistically be little likelihood of our meeting again in the future. If that is so, we have to ask ourselves why it is important to us to maintain these old friendships. Surely it would be better to say that they were good while we were in close contact, but that now we have all moved on. We are no longer part of their lives, as they are no longer part of ours. Let us remember the friendship with gratitude and some regret at its ending, and leave it at that.

One reason why I am unwilling to do this is because I find that the original attraction of personalities in a friendship lasts, and goes on lasting, irrespective of geographical separation and the infrequency of our meetings. According to the Myers-Briggs personality assessment tests, I am of an extrovert disposition. As I look at my friends, I recognise that many are just the opposite. It is an attraction of opposites. There is a balance and affection in our relationship which is tacitly recognised and expressed in the understanding we offer one another. This understanding includes several distinct qualities, the most important of which is openness. With my oldest friends, I dare to be open, to tell them what I really feel. When we meet and they ask me how I am, I know them well enough to confide in them the real answer to their question, rather than the social convention of assurance that I am fine. This involves trust, and the assurance of acceptance. It involves laying the burden of self-revelation on our friends, but we would not be willing to do that unless we felt that our relationship was able to bear the weight. In doing so, we become aware of a paradox: the relationship, instead of showing signs of the strain which we place upon it, will in the end be stronger because of it.

There is also another paradox. We find that old friendships, established across the years, withstand the separation of time and distance. Indeed, those that do not were perhaps never true friendships. When we meet up again with old friends, we carry on as we did before. There is no difficulty, no awkwardness. We recognise what first attracted us and brought us together. Now we give it new impetus and it is strengthened. If I were to abandon that friendship, I would experience a real sense of loss, and feel diminished as a person.

Those whom Jesus called to be with him were disciples. They travelled with him, sat at his feet to be instructed by his teaching, and absorbed his message through the experiences of his ministry in which they shared. They also became his friends: "You are my friends if you do what I command you." In return, Jesus expressed his friendship with them in the highest possible terms, anticipating what lay ahead of him: "No one has greater love than this, to lay down one's life for one's friends." With these words, Jesus defines our relationship with God. Through the dying and rising of Jesus, we are able, with the greatest possible reverence, to call God our friend. This is not without parallel in human terms. It is a great blessing for parents and children to be able to regard one another as friends as well.

Our friendship with God may have become distant over the years, but because of God's loving persistence, it is never allowed to lapse entirely, or become completely broken. Later life can be a good time to renew, restore and repair that relationship, so that we can once again be close with God, and know that presence in every aspect of our lives. It is a closeness, a friendship, that can be with us now, and still remain to be explored and enjoyed in all its fullness in the nearer presence of God.

Heavenly Father,
we give thanks
for the friendships that we have formed,
for the acceptance and understanding
that has nourished us and sustained us
across the years,
and that now withstands
separation by distance,
and the passage of time.
May we know such closeness
and friendship with you
through your Son, Jesus Christ,
that will enrich the life we live now,
and bring us fulfilment in your presence
in the life that is to come. Amen.

Independence

At the time of writing, I am still fully independent. Creaky knees remind me of the passage of time, but apart from that, I am thankful to be fit and well, and, above all, independent.

As we progress into later life, it is increasingly important for us to remain independent for as long as we can. Indeed, the older we grow, the more valuable our independence becomes, and the more some of us need to prove that we can manage alone and unaided. When I took the car to the garage for its annual service and MOT, the garage offered to clean the car, both inside and out, as part of the deal. At that time, there had been a lot of rain, the roads were muddy, and, as a consequence, the car was really dirty. Even though I knew the garage would clean it as a matter of routine, it offended my sense of independence that I should let them do this for me, and, further, that I should be glad to let them do it. I was perfectly able to clean the car myself – so I did, and my car went for its service and complimentary clean shining and spotless! I was not looking for another tedious job, but neither was I willing to let someone else do it for me who might have thought that because the car was so dirty I was getting past it. Here was a classic case of old-age pride and self-esteem getting mixed up with the need to prove my independence to no one else but myself.

I recognise that I am equally ambivalent in other areas of life. I am happy to be told what is going to happen by one of our children, all now in their forties, and all of them very competent organisers. It is a welcome relief to know that all my wife and I have to do is to turn up and enjoy the occasion that they have arranged, without any of the responsibility involved in the preparation. It is also comforting to have confidence that the arrangements will go smoothly and, except for unforeseen circumstances, will proceed without a hitch. But I am aware that, in gladly accepting all of this, we are, to some extent, handing over the independence that we have known and exercised as parents.

Perhaps it is with this realisation that anxiety begins to creep in, an anxiety that probably most of us share in some form or another: what will happen to us when the day comes, for whatever reason, when we lose our independence? The prospect is not an appealing one. Indeed, it is extremely frightening, and we have no desire to dwell upon it. Yet inevitably it is there, and perhaps one day I shall be saying, as so many people have said to me in the past, "I don't want to be a burden to the family." The family usually deprecate the idea – "Of course you won't. We're here to look after you." But things do not always work out that way, and added to the burden of losing one's independence is the knowledge that this may lay great stress on the family, and be the source of difficult and strained relationships.

Some of Jesus' last words to Peter resonate for us in later life: "When you were younger, you used to fasten you own belt and go wherever you wished. But when you grow old, you will stretch out your hands, and someone else will fasten a belt around you and take you where you do not wish to go." We gather from the Gospels that Peter was an extrovert character. Often he seems to have spoken first and thought second. "Go away from me, Lord," was his first reaction to the great catch of fish, "for I am a sinful man." Such impetuosity can be difficult to deal with, but it is far better to speak out and communicate our needs, our hopes and fears, to those who are near and dear to us, rather than suffer in silence. That kind of silence will only add to their pain and ours. They need to know how we feel about the loss of our independence, or the prospect of that happening. They are concerned for us, look after us, and ultimately are going to be very much involved in the decisions about our care.

It may be difficult, both for them and for ourselves, if we are moving into new territory, areas of mutual communication into which none of us has ventured before. Perhaps they will need our help, just as much as we need theirs. In this way, paradoxically, we may find that we are maintaining our inner independence just at the time when our external independence is slipping from our grasp.

Our ultimate fear must be the total loss of independence through the onset of senility, and the disintegration of our dignity and personality. If we reach the point where total darkness descends, it will be worse for our loved ones than for us. They will need to cling on to the words of Psalm 139 to sustain them: "Even the darkness is not dark to you; the night is as clear as the day, for darkness is as light to you."

Ultimately, our personality, our dignity, and our independence rest with God and in God. We are known and loved and nurtured by God to the end.

> *Heavenly Father,*
> *ever-present in our lives;*
> *as increasing years bring us*
> *greater dependence on those around us,*
> *may they also bring us*
> *greater dependence on you.*
> *Grant us to know*
> *that true independence*
> *comes from you*
> *and is found in you,*   *.*
> *and that you sustain us*
> *to the end,*
> *in your Son, Jesus Christ our Lord. Amen.*

Emotional fly-tipping

My wife and I live in a small 1960s development, built on the site of three Victorian villas which these days would have been preserved. Behind the houses is a line of garages, and a cul-de-sac where no one visits much and no one sees what is going on. Occasionally, groups of under-age children gather there to smoke their cigarettes, but – much worse – the area has become the target of fly-tippers. Garden rubbish we can cope with and get rid of fairly easily, but concrete and brick-ends demand professional removal, and that costs money. Fly-tipping is a common problem, and some people have suffered far more seriously than we have on our small estate up to now.

However, fly-tipping takes place metaphorically as well as literally, and we are all guilty of it from time to time. It is easy to offload our feelings on to those who are nearest and dearest to us. When we are in a bad mood, sometimes we actively look for trouble. We pick an argument on the slightest pretext, and make life difficult for those around us. In a sense, we are fly-tipping emotionally. We are dumping our emotions, our bad feelings, on other people. In some situations there may be no one conveniently at hand on to whom we can safely discharge our feelings. So we have to recognise them for what they are, and the destruction they can cause. We have to treat ourselves gently, and develop suitable coping strategies. Ultimately all this is true, whether we live alone, with someone else, or with others whom we know and trust.

The desire to fly-tip emotionally makes itself apparent in many areas of life, increasingly so, it seems, and sometimes with disastrous consequences. "Road rage" has been known to end in the death of one of the people involved. "Trolley rage" is not unknown as we try to find the checkout with the shortest queue at the supermarket, and woe betide anyone who seeks to push in ahead of us in the long-established British custom of queuing. On the day I write these words, the newspaper headline protests at "word rage"; the choice of words used by a leading politician has caused deep offence in some sections of the community. And I have my own particular rage, directed against cyclists who pedal at speed along the pavement. They make me feel threatened and extremely vulnerable. But I also rage at my own impotence in the face of this threat to my life and limb, and my inability to do anything about it. I recognise the strength of my feelings. I do my best to absorb them, and not to offload them. I know how destructive this kind of "fly-tipping" can be.

We find the same dynamic at work as we read the Bible. In the opening chapters, Cain rages at his brother Abel. He is so violently jealous, that he takes Abel out into the field, and murders him there. Even before that, we find Adam and Eve offloading their personal responsibility for having eaten the forbidden fruit in the Garden of Eden, and discharging their sense of guilt. Adam blames Eve, and Eve blames the serpent. The psalmists frequently express the frustrated and bewildered feelings of the Jewish people against "the wicked" – those who have turned their back on God, and seem to get away with it: "I was envious of the arrogant; I saw the prosperity of the wicked." Even Psalm 139 to which I return time and again contains this curse: "O that you would kill the wicked, O God, ... those who speak of you maliciously, and lift themselves up against you for evil!" St Paul admitted that he was speaking as a fool when he boasted angrily of his achievements, as he wrote to the Church at Corinth, and elsewhere he vented his anger on what he called the "foolish Galatians". The parable of the Good Samaritan was a response to the lawyer who had "stood up to test Jesus", and then asked him a further question "wanting to justify himself". But Jesus did not "offload" his anger; it was directed righteously and spontaneously against those who deserved it. So Mark tells us that he was angry with those who doubted his ability to heal the man with the withered arm, and "was grieved at their hardness of heart". He was even more grieved by those who had turned his "Father's house into a market place". "Take these things out of here!" he cried as he drove the dealers, tradespeople and money changers from the Temple in Jerusalem. Violent as those words were, they were not an expression of Jesus' own anger, but of his claims for the righteousness of God. The cry of dereliction – "My God, my God, why have you forsaken me?" – as Jesus hung upon the cross is perhaps the only glimpse we have of Jesus' personal anger and revulsion at the hideous and agonising death to which he was being subjected. Yet even this expression of Jesus' inner tumult is not directed against those who have caused his suffering. It is a cry to his Father, a moment from the depths shared with him alone, and Jesus dies with compassion in his heart and on his lips: "Father, forgive them; for they do not know what they are doing." St Peter summed up the moment in his first letter: "When he was abused, he did not return abuse; when he suffered, he did not threaten."

That is an ideal we find it hard to live up to. It is difficult to know how to deal with our accumulation of emotional waste. We do not want it – and nor does anyone else. Above all, we must not indulge in emotional fly-tipping. There are no easy answers, but an old hymn does at least suggest one: *"Bringing all my burdens, Sorrow, sin and care, At thy feet I lay them, And I leave them there."*

Eternal Father,
we give you thanks
that in Jesus you accept us as we are.
Give us grace, patience and wisdom
to accept others as they are,
and not to lay upon them
our anger, our frustrations and our fears,
but to leave our burdens
at the foot of the cross
of your Son, our Saviour, Jesus Christ. Amen.

Touch

One day, I passed two young mothers standing talking together on the street corner, small children dozing in pushchairs. I overheard one saying to the other, "My mum never touched me. She never picked me up, or gave me a cuddle, or anything like that." My first reaction as I passed by was – how sad. As I walked on further, I began to reflect on the importance of touch.

Touch is a vital means of communication, or, more precisely, non-verbal communication. The story is told of Archbishop Thomas Cranmer at the bedside of the dying Henry VIII. Henry was far gone, but, in one of his waking moments, Cranmer asked him if he wished to seek forgiveness for all that he had done wrong. If so, he was to squeeze Cranmer's hand. The squeeze, faint as it was, duly came, and Cranmer pronounced absolution. I have sat by the bedside of many ill people, holding their hands until the moment of death. They were beyond words, either to speak themselves, or to hear anything that I might say, even though hearing is reputed to be the last of the human faculties to be lost. But touch was still possible, and that I maintained to the last. Touch is important for those who, in every sense, handle people, and especially those who are ill. I can remember a patient saying to me years ago that you could always tell a good nurse by the way they touched you and handled you. The same, I am sure, is true of all the caring professions, and in all our relationships and dealings with one another.

We communicate so many things through touch. Touch conveys warmth, both physical and emotional, qualities which are so essential for the well-being of a child. Perhaps the young mother I overheard was acknowledging her inability to offer her children the touch which she instinctively recognised was so important because she herself had been deprived of it in her own childhood. As well as warmth, touch carries with it the expression of comfort, closeness, affirmation and understanding, qualities which produce and sustain our feelings of well-being in life, whatever age we may be.

We need the affirmation of the caring touch, both physically and emotionally. We can find ourselves "touched", sometimes quite profoundly, by people's words, thoughtfulness, acts of kindness, the willingness and ability of others to put themselves in someone else's place, and to understand all that that means. It carries with it something intrinsically healing – the healing touch, indeed. I have always found the healing of the woman who had suffered haemorrhages for many years, to be one of the most compelling in the Gospels. Jesus is surrounded by a large crowd, actually on his way to lay hands on the daughter of Jairus, one of the leaders of the local synagogue. The woman pushes through the crowd: "'If I but touch his clothes, I will be made well' ... Immediately aware that power had gone forth from him, Jesus turned about in the crowd and said, 'Who touched my clothes?'" It seemed an impossible question with so many people surrounding him, yet Jesus was aware of the significance of this special touch, both to himself and the woman.

We belong to a generation which was brought up not to touch, and now finds it difficult to touch. We have been reluctant to touch other people except in a formally distanced kind of way. Now, late in life, I believe we are at long last getting used to the idea of actually daring to make physical contact, and getting better at putting it into practice – even though there remains a lingering unease with sharing the peace within the Eucharist. Every day, we touch each other in all sorts of ways, emotionally as well as physically, perhaps even just being with people, and our touch can carry with it the quality of healing. I am reminded of the words of an old hymn:

"We touch him in life's throng and press
And we are whole again."

In later life, when our own touch is gradually becoming less
confident and certain than it once was, we too need the reassurance
of the affirming touch from those who are closest to us.

> *Heavenly Father,*
> *in his earthly ministry*
> *your Son touched those in need,*
> *bringing to them healing for the present,*
> *and hope for the future.*
> *Enable us to continue his ministry,*
> *so that, in later life,*
> *by physical presence,*
> *and sympathetic understanding,*
> *we may bring his touch*
> *to those who need his healing*
> *in their lives.*
> *We ask this for his name's sake. Amen.*

Christmas presents

Each year, we rack our brains as to what presents we can buy for one another at Christmas. No matter how early we start, the process seems to go on for ever, and the decisions get no easier. Buying presents for children can be particularly difficult. We really want to buy them something – the pleasure is ours, and we hope it will be theirs as well. But sometimes we are left wondering whether our children receive more presents than they can comfortably cope with, and whether the effort on our part was really worthwhile. Our minds may go back to the times when there was no long commercial run-up to Christmas, and Santa Claus did not arrive in the shops at the end of October. Festivities were confined to a few days, and presents were more modest than they are now.

Perhaps because of the wide choice available, children can be unpredictable as to what they will like, or what will actually engage their attention. The present we choose for them may not appeal at all. They may be taken instead with something we bought for their sibling, or something we bought as an afterthought, just a stocking-filler. Perhaps really young children will most enjoy the wrapping itself, crumpling the paper and discovering what it tastes like!

In spite of these yearly problems with choosing suitable presents we are happy to regard Christmas as a time for children, observing in later life that we are all children at heart. It is interesting, therefore, that a close reading of the Christmas story reveals that most of the people involved were old rather than young. The narrative begins with the appearance of the angel to Zechariah as he performs his duties at the altar of incense in the sanctuary. The angel tells him that in spite of the fact that "Elizabeth was barren, and both were getting on in years", they would have a child who was to be named

John. (In the fullness of time, he would become the Baptist.) Christian tradition has it that although Mary was young, possibly still in her teens, Joseph was somewhat older. When he and Mary took the infant Jesus to be presented at the Temple in Jerusalem, they were greeted there by Simeon, a "religious and devout" man. "It had been revealed to him by the Holy Spirit that he would not see death before he had seen the Lord's Messiah." It seems reasonable to assume that he too was "getting on in years". Anna the prophet was even older, having reached the age of eighty-four. "She never left the temple but worshipped there with fasting and prayer night and day." She, too, greeted the Christ child, as did the wise men after their long journey. Perhaps they had accumulated over a long period of years the wisdom to search for and find the Christ child, the wealth to provide the gifts they brought him, and the experience to out-manoeuvre the manipulation and treachery of Herod. All these people, in their own particular way, offered their personal gifts to the infant Christ. They remind us that although the baby was the pivotal character, the story would not have developed as it did without the contribution of people in their third age. They also remind us that the most precious and lasting gifts we can give our children are the intangible ones: gifts of love, warmth, understanding, comfort, reassurance, forgiveness, acceptance.

It is easy to take such gifts for granted, and to assume that they will form a natural part of children's lives. That is by no means the case. The children's charities constantly remind us that there is still much social deprivation of which children are often the main victims. Even worse, there are many instances of outright cruelty towards children. There is a public outcry when such cases are reported and brought to court, but many are not, and are concealed from public attention. From time to time, as I go about, I see children being verbally abused instead of being comforted, reassured and listened to. Often it seems that their parents are young and inexperienced. Perhaps they never knew or enjoyed those inner gifts which would have created their own confidence and self-esteem. It is understandable that they have little to pass on to their own children, when they are little more than children themselves.

In later life, we may all fulfil a number of roles in our children's lives, as grandparents (perhaps even great-grandparents), godparents, great-aunts and great-uncles, neighbours, friends of the family. The gifts we are able to contribute are not confined to Christmas. They are gifts which overflow any timescale or seasonal package. Perhaps we may live long enough to see them come to fruition in the young lives of the rising generation, with all their spontaneity and unpredictability. Thank God for the gift of spontaneity and unpredictability. Thank God for the gift of the Christ child, and for the gifts we are able to share with one another.

> *Father, we give thanks*
> *for all your gifts towards us,*
> *especially the gift of Jesus your Son,*
> *born amongst us*
> *as a child in the manger.*
> *Of the gifts that we give our children,*
> *at Christmas and throughout the year,*
> *may we value most*
> *those that will enable them*
> *to be loved, valued, esteemed, and accepted,*
> *after the pattern of your Son,*
> *Jesus Christ, our Lord. Amen.*

Aloneness

My wife and I attended the funeral of a very old friend, someone we had known for over fifty years. He was a popular man – "Uncle Bob" not only to his own nephews and nieces, but also to many other children over the years, including our own. He enjoyed life to the full, a great sportsman and a man of many talents, he pursued many interests with great enthusiasm. He was a founder member of his local church which was filled to capacity for his funeral, a joyful service with warm tributes and a genuine thanksgiving for his life. Bob had always been a member of the choir, so we sang some rousing hymns of which he would have approved.

It was all so different when we arrived at the crematorium. It was one of the older ones, built in a style that was gaunt and severe. The chapel was long and narrow, and the coffin lay at the far end, as far removed from the congregation as it possibly could be. We were separated not only physically and geographically, but, it felt, spiritually and emotionally as well. It was such a contrast from the church, where we were gathering round an old friend to take our leave and bid him farewell. Now he was very much on his own.

This separation reminded me forcibly of the words from the funeral service which I had pronounced so many times over the years: "We brought nothing into the world, and we take nothing out. The Lord gives, and the Lord takes away: blessed be the name of the Lord." The solemnity of these words carries increasing meaning as we progress into our third age. There are two moments in life which each of us has to pass through alone. These are the moments of birth and death. As soon as we are born, we are wrapped up and enveloped, both literally and metaphorically, cared for, and, all being well, loved and nurtured. But the journey from the womb and our entry into the world, we have to accomplish alone. Similarly at the end of life. It would be good to think that those whom we knew and loved were watching and waiting with us as death approached. But the journey through death and into whatever lies beyond, we have to accomplish alone.

However, aloneness is not confined to birth and death, the extremities of life. Many of us carry aloneness with us all through our lives. It is an integral part of our being. For some, it represents a safety zone, a welcome space deep within us, where we can retreat from the stresses of life which press in upon us day by day. We emerge, in our own time, feeling refreshed and renewed, our batteries re-charged. For others, aloneness may be a no-go area, marked, as such areas are, with terrible signs and dire warnings which tell us to keep away. The former battlefields of our world are still littered with unexploded live ammunition that threatens life and limb. Equally destructive forces may still be at work within the aloneness of many of us.

In his poem "Ambulances", Philip Larkin writes of "the solving emptiness that lies just under all we do". The "solving emptiness" belongs to us, each one individually, and to us alone. It is not an area easily reached, experienced or shared, even with those closest to us. Our "solving emptiness" may lie beyond words. Yet whether the experience is positive or negative, our essential aloneness does not lie beyond God. Indeed, it is in that essential aloneness that we find and are closest to God. So at the deepest level of our being, we find the Christian paradox at work: when we are most essentially alone, we are not alone, for in that aloneness, God is most truly with us.

"Out of the depths I cry to you, O Lord," writes the Psalmist. We have confidence that God is with us in the deepest part of our being, and will hear our call.

Father,
your Son, Jesus Christ,
sought moments apart
to be alone
for quiet reflection
and to renew his oneness with you.
Be with us, we pray,
in the depths of our being.
May we draw strength
from what is good within us,
and may we find healing
amid the wounds that hurt us still.
When we call to you
from the depths of our aloneness,
be near to us, and hear our cry.
We ask this in the name of Jesus Christ, our Lord.
  Amen.

Bad news

According to the old saying, "no news is good news", but as I write, there seems to be no good news at all. There are "wars and rumours of wars". Terrorism strikes worldwide, violence seems to be endemic in our society, and global warming is a major concern. We live with a constant stream of bad news to the point where we become immune to it, and de-sensitised by it. We do feel genuinely sad for those who are caught up in traumatic events, and suffer grievous personal loss, but inevitably it is in an exterior kind of way. So often we are left asking ourselves what we can do to help remedy the situation, and bring about some kind of relief. The only way seems to be to contribute to yet another appeal for money. Yet even the major international charities and relief agencies recognise a "compassion fatigue" after so many appeals to respond to a succession of crises. There is no lack of goodwill on our part. We do not wish to "pass by on the other side". Yet the scale of the bad news that assails us leaves us feeling that we cannot afford, for our own well-being and personal survival, to take on our shoulders the whole burden of suffering humanity. We should never survive if we did.

Really bad news for us personally may not be news at all on a level or on a scale that gets reported by the news media. It is learning of things which affect us deeply, personally, adversely. Each one of us will respond to those words according to our own experience of life. It could be that what we thought and expected was financially secure has suddenly disappeared. The onset of physical or mental frailty may mean that we are unable to maintain an independent lifestyle any longer, or at least that we have to "downsize". We suffer the loss of familiar surroundings and personal effects that have been with us for years and have formed the setting within which we have lived our lives. Bad news can include serious or debilitating illness, in ourselves or those who are close to us. Almost certainly, the worst news of all is to learn of the death of someone we know and love, someone who has been part of our life over the years. All of us in later life will be familiar with that feeling. As we grow older, the experience of receiving bad news, the experience of loss, becomes more frequent. We may well wonder whether the next bad news to be circulated will involve our own departure from this life, or whether the day will come when we are left alone, in the sense that all our contemporaries have died, and we are the sole survivors of our generation.

It is difficult at any stage of life to cope with the bad news of the death of someone who is close to us, someone whom we have known and loved. Even in our third age, our long experience of life is not in itself sufficient to compensate for offsetting the bad news we have received, and now have to cope with. The daily routine can be an antidote, even though we may have little energy, little enthusiasm for keeping things going. Working through bereavement is an exhausting process. We have that much less emotional energy in later life, and the impact is that much greater.

There are many biblical texts which are used to try to lessen and absorb the impact of death: "Underneath are the everlasting arms," is one from the book of Deuteronomy, and another from St John's Gospel: "Do not let your hearts be troubled ... in my Father's house are many dwelling-places." But such words, well intentioned as they are, may not be able to penetrate the wall of bad news in order to resonate within us. St Paul knew troubles enough during his travels, and had to cope with instances of bad news from many different quarters. So I find myself much more in sympathy with the words that he wrote in his letter to the Church at Rome: "I am convinced that neither death nor life ... nor anything else in all creation will be able to separate us from the love of God in Christ

Jesus our Lord." In other words, when we receive bad news, there is no need to struggle or load ourselves with the effort of pretending that we are "all right". We can admit the pain, the grief, the sense of loss, the emptiness and utter weariness, knowing that God is with us, loves us, accepts us, expects nothing more from us than what we are. In the person of Jesus, he knows our human condition, and experienced it for himself. Jesus' friend Lazarus fell ill and died. When he reached Bethany, and saw the tomb where Lazarus had been laid, "Jesus began to weep." He ordered the stone to be removed from the mouth of the cave, and "cried with a loud voice, 'Lazarus, come out!' The dead man came out, his hands and feet bound with strips of cloth and his face wrapped in a cloth. Jesus said to them, 'Unbind him, and let him go.'" I quote these verses in full, because I believe the imagery is important for us. We, too, are bound – paralysed, in a sense – when we receive the bad news of a loved one's death. Lazarus was unbound immediately. It will take us much longer to feel free to take up the normality of life again. But recalling Paul's words, we can rest assured of our acceptance by God on every step we make to recovery, in whatever way we may choose to do it, and in whatever direction it may take us.

Nor do we forget that Jesus ordered the stone to be rolled away. It was a sign of resurrection, of life after death, and looked forward to his own. No matter how bad the news may have been, no matter how much devastation the impact has caused on our lives, here is the outward sign of God's assurance that we can, at some point, begin to look forward again. We can dare to contemplate the future. We can begin to live once more. Neither death nor life, nor indeed, any news, no matter how bad, can separate us from the loving acceptance that God has promised us, and opened to us in his Son, Jesus Christ our Lord.

Father,
when we are surrounded by bad news
in the world that you have made,
take away despair, and give us hope.
When bad news strikes our lives
and we are faced with the death
of those near and dear,
enable us to rest on the acceptance of your love,
and your assurance of the gift of life,
    now and for ever. Amen.

Our own mortality

"Depend upon it, Sir," said Dr Johnson, the eighteenth-century English writer, of a contemporary who was soon to be executed, "when a man knows he is to be hanged in a fortnight, it concentrates his mind wonderfully." The minds of my wife and myself were very much concentrated by the deaths of two very old friends within a few days of each other. Two months later, another old friend died, and two months after that, yet another. They were all friends of forty or fifty years' standing, and although we had not met recently because of distance, our friendship survived the periods of separation and was fresh and long-lasting. From the point of view of age, they were all our contemporaries within a year or two.

So we were reminded again of our own mortality. (The one inescapable fact of being in one's third age is that there is far less life to come than has already passed.) What took our attention was not how or when we might die, over which we have no control, but what happens afterwards for those we leave behind, over which we do have some control – our wills, and the arrangements for our funerals. Hidden in the Order for the Visitation of the Sick in the Book of Common Prayer, is the instruction that if the sick person "hath not before disposed of his goods, let him then be admonished to make his Will". Even if our will is drawn up in the briefest and simplest terms, we need to remember that it is a legal document, and that its legality needs to be established beyond question. The charge for doing this is not great, and is well worth the sense of relief that it brings to know that we have set down clearly and legally how we wish to dispose of our worldly goods, no matter how modest they may be. Having done that, we need to keep our will under review. Circumstances change over the years, and what was appropriate when we drew it up may no longer be so with the inevitable passage of time. So, as you read these words, in whatever state of health you find yourself, let me encourage you, rather than "admonish" you, to make your will, if you have not already done so: legally, officially, and with the help of a solicitor.

It is also helpful to our families and friends to give them some indication regarding the arrangements for our funeral. Families expend so much time and emotional energy trying to make difficult decisions which only make a difficult time even worse. So we need to tell them whether we wish to be buried or cremated. If we choose burial, where is the grave to be? If we choose cremation, what is to happen to the ashes? Are they to be buried or scattered? In either case, the family need to know where. Have we any preferences as to who might officiate at our funeral? If so, do they know about it? Have we any choice regarding hymns or readings? Are there to be flowers, or donations in lieu? If so, to what good cause? So the list goes on. But if we can deal with this list, and tell our family and friends, it forms a valuable part of our legacy to them. The funeral is, in the best possible sense, for them, not for us, and we want to help them all we can, just as we have always done. A notice that says, "No flowers by request. Donations to be sent to ..." is helpful. Everyone knows where they stand. But I remember seeing a notice that said, "No funeral. No flowers. No friends. No fuss." I thought it was extremely sad. I knew the man was a non-believer and that he was single with no relatives or even distant family. But I also knew that there were people who considered themselves to be his friends, and they needed their opportunity to make their farewell.

As we look at the Gospels, we can see that, even at a relatively early stage in his ministry, Jesus was beginning to prepare for his death. At Jesus' transfiguration, Moses and Elijah "appeared in glory and were speaking of his departure, which he was about to accomplish in Jerusalem". Jesus saw his death as completing and fulfilling his mission. Yet even as he hung upon the cross, one last piece of "unfinished business" demanded his attention. "When Jesus saw his mother and the disciple whom he loved standing beside her, he said to his mother, 'Woman, here is your son.' Then he said to the disciple, 'Here is your mother.' And from that hour the disciple took her into his own home." Only then could Jesus cry, "It is finished" and surrender himself to death. "Father, into your hands I commend my spirit." Having said this, he breathed his last.

There cannot be many of us who are able to arrange our departure at the end of life in such a measured way. Taking leave, saying goodbye, especially for the last time, is always painful; it can be no other. We want to ease the pain of our parting as much as we can for those whom we know and love. Indeed, we owe it to them. It is this that should concentrate our minds, and we can find a wonderful sense of completion and fulfilment when everything is arranged as we want it to be. "Lord, now lettest thou thy servant depart in peace."

> *Father,*
> *give us, we pray,*
> *courage and faith*
> *to follow the example of your Son,*
> *who in the midst of life*
> *prepared for death,*
> *so that we may ease*
> *the pain of parting*
> *for those whom we leave behind,*
> *and ourselves be content*
> *to depart in peace*
> *to be with you for ever. Amen.*

D**** (The word we avoid)

When I was in the army doing my national service, four-letter words were commonplace. They were used on the parade ground, in our all-too-frequent kit inspections, and in the barrack room. They were used in conversation generally, mostly by young men of limited vocabulary, who needed the recourse to four-letter words in order to express themselves adequately. Fifty years on, four-letter words have become part of our everyday speech, used on a regular basis by people at every level of society. They are used in advertising, appear in graffiti, and are known and apparently understood by children of – to me – tender years. Given this robustness in our use of language, it seems ironic that a five-letter word causes far more difficulty. We fight shy of it, and find it difficult to use, especially in relation to ourselves. Yet there is only one certainty in life. Once we are born, we move steadily towards death.

We would find it helpful if only we knew more about it, and what to expect. How do we experience death, and what is it like to die? Yet no one can tell us, and the Bible, where we might think to find at least some kind of answer, has little to say on the subject. The emphasis in the Gospels is on preparation for the second coming of Christ on the last day, when the kingdom of God will ultimately be established. Entry into the kingdom will involve judgement on the basis of how we have lived this life as a preparation for the life to come.

Judgement – the separation of the good from the bad – is graphically described in the parable of the sheep and the goats in St Matthew's Gospel. It is a scene which was depicted in murals over the chancel arch in many ancient churches. Some of the paintings have survived, and we can see for ourselves the power and the ferocity of the uncompromising message which they convey. St Paul used a different imagery. He writes in his first letter to the Thessalonians, "For the Lord himself, with a cry of command … and with the sound of God's trumpet, will descend from heaven, and the dead in Christ will rise first." But this is still in the realm of poetry, seeking to express the inexpressible. Jairus' daughter, the son of the widow at Nain, and Lazarus were all restored to life by Jesus: we could wish that they had described and handed on their experience, so that we could know what really happens, and what to expect, when we die.

Perhaps the closest we can come to this is the body of evidence provided by people who have passed through near-death experiences. However, because these are, and can only be, subjective, it is difficult to apply to them the rigorous disciplines of scientific research in order to establish their authenticity. I have been with dying people who have apparently been aware of family members and friends, themselves departed from this life, waiting round the bed to welcome the dying person into their midst. I have heard this same story repeated from other sources, too often to be able to dismiss it merely as folklore, wishful thinking, or a figment of the imagination. During the course of my ministry, I have formed the impression that the dividing line, "the veil", the partition, whatever we like to call it, between this life and whatever lies beyond, becomes transparently thin at the point of death.

But in writing these things, I am aware that I can only be speculating, like so many other people. Even those who are convinced that death is the end, and that there is nothing more beyond, are speculating in their own way. So, believing that death is not the end, let me offer a couple of suggestions as we think about our own death, and wonder what it might be like. One is on a purely physical level. Going to sleep each night is a kind of dying, a mini-death. We assume we shall wake up in the morning, and perhaps take it for granted that another day will open out ahead of us. But if we see this simple process in terms of an act of faith, because there is no certainty that the new day will dawn, or that we shall live to see it, then the new day is a gift from God, and something to be thankful for. It is a moment of resurrection.

Death and resurrection have their place on an emotional level as well. Each day can bring us hurts, disappointments, personal failures, inner as well as outer conflicts, turmoil of the soul. All these represent mini-deaths. Something within us dies. But, there is also resurrection: when an apology is made and accepted, when there is understanding and forgiveness, reconciliation and healing. People can offer us such grace and graciousness, that they make us feel good. We blossom in their presence. They offer us life, and, by being with them, we come alive again.

In their finality and fullness, death and resurrection await us at the end of our lives. But to some degree, at least, they are with us already. Dying and rising are an essential element of daily life. And – who knows? – possibly, just possibly, how we cope with death and resurrection when the moment comes will depend on how we have coped with death and resurrection in the here and now.

> *Lord of life,*
> *and conqueror of death,*
> *we give thanks*
> *that you have led us*
> *on the path of life.*
> *We pray that as we have known death and*
> *resurrection in our lives day by day,*
> *so we may pass through death*
> *to the fullness of the resurrection*
> *which you have made known to us*
> *in your Son, Jesus Christ our Lord. Amen.*

Unfinished business

Some thirty years ago, my father lay dying of cancer. As a family, we had never talked with him about the inevitable outcome of his illness, nor he with us. Each one of the family knew, I am sure my father knew, but no one spoke openly, or even dared to do so.

My father was a very private man, very reserved, and never spoke of his feelings. This may have been something to do with his experiences in the First World War, where, barely aged twenty, he had been caught up in the Battle of the Somme. I suppose it is true to say that whatever degree of closeness I shared with him as a child was replaced by a withdrawal into mutual reserve as I got older. As I look back, I think both of us were aware of our feelings for the other, but lacked the means or the courage to express them. The prospect of his imminent death formed, for me at least, an even more impenetrable barrier between us. With hindsight, he was more aware of it than I was. I went to see him for what I think both of us knew would be the last time. I cannot now remember what we talked about, but I do remember, vividly and unhappily, the moment I got up to go. Out of the blue, he said to me, "Have you anything else you want to say to me?" I am sure he was doing his best to let me know that he knew what the situation was, and to use those last few moments to round things off. Maybe he was giving me the opportunity to say goodbye, and to help him do the same. But the question was so much out of character, and it took me so much by surprise, that I could only answer "No." At that moment, it was a truthful reply. I had not read his signal, and, on the spur of the moment, I could not think of anything else I wanted to say. Perhaps if I had been quicker and more collected, I might have returned the question: had he anything that he wanted to say to me? But I don't think that I would have been willing to risk the embarrassment that might have ensued for both of us by venturing into unknown territory, especially at this late stage. It was probably too late for both of us by then.

Over the years, I have regretted so often my reply, its inaccuracy, and the moment of essential untruthfulness. My father and I both had so much unfinished business with each other. Indeed, we had never really started. Now I have the lasting regret that I know so little about him, and the kind of person that he really was, and not just as I perceived him as a child. In what now seems a strange kind of way, we kept our distance, almost by tacit mutual consent, never really touching each other, either literally or metaphorically. As I have now reached the age my father was when he died, the realisation of what we both missed in our relationship with each other is a nagging source of sadness and regret.

I have taken this substantial piece of unfinished business with me into my third age. It is too late to do anything about it, and, humanly speaking, my father will never know what lasting effect his death has had upon me. But it does at least have the positive effect of reminding me not to leave other such items of unfinished business until it is too late. There are people with whom I must renew contact, friends to visit, family ties to renew. There may be the need for explanations, the need to make amends, the need for mutual forgiveness. We do not wish to leave people we have known and loved with lasting regrets. We do not wish to leave them with unfinished business as far as we are concerned, any more than we want it for ourselves.

In the opening verses of the Acts of the Apostles, the disciples ask Jesus to give them some indication as to when God will bring about the restoration of the kingdom to Israel. His answer was to remind them of the fragility of life. "It is not for you to know the times or periods that the Father has set by his own authority." Several parables carried the same message. Jesus told of the rich businessman who looked forward to a secure and prosperous future, with his barns full of produce, and no material worries of any kind. He would "relax, eat, drink, be merry". But God said to him, "You fool! This very night your life is being demanded of you. And the things you have prepared, whose will they be?" This is the question which demands the attention of those of us in later life, and we need to be able to make a satisfactory reply. The situation is summed up in a verse from the letter to the Ephesians: "Be careful how you live, not as unwise people but as wise, making the most of the time." They are wise words at any stage of life. In our third age, we must make the most of our time.

Lord of life,
and creator of time,
we give thanks
for the time you have given us
to enjoy our life in your world.
Give us the courage to acknowledge
that our time on earth is limited,
and the courage to complete our affairs,
so that nothing is outstanding.
May we rest content
that all that needs to be done
has been done,
and that we can come before you
knowing that we have been wise
in using our time and yours
in the service of your Son,
Jesus Christ our Lord. Amen.

Vulnerability

A surprising statistic is that more accidents occur in the safe surroundings of our homes than on our busy and often congested roads. I became one of those statistics when I fell off a stepladder and broke my arm. Fortunately, it was a simple break, and the consultant at our local hospital considered it sufficient to give me a collar and cuff, and let the break heal itself. A collar and cuff, for those who have never worn one, is a length of lint-covered plastic foam looped round the neck and forearm, the former thus supporting the latter. It is a simple but ingenious arrangement, which in my case worked well. At first, I felt conspicuous and vulnerable. However, I soon learned that the collar and cuff acted as a kind of safety measure. It was a visible signal that I was, at least temporarily, a casualty. People recognised that, and instinctively, it seemed, gave me a little more space. The moment that really scared me was when the consultant told me that my arm had mended well, and that I no longer needed the support of my collar and cuff. He took it off and threw it away. I then had to face the world without a signal that I was carrying an injury – mending fast, but nevertheless still there, and one of which I felt very much aware.

Even in my usual robust health, there are times when I feel vulnerable. I am not a small man. I am over six feet tall and well-built, but I can still feel dwarfed and somewhat intimidated by the sheer size of many young people, their physical exuberance and sometimes, it has to be said, their choice of language. I try not to be around in the afternoon when the schools finish their day, and discharge their pupils onto the streets around where we live and into our local shopping centre. Sometimes our vulnerability is evident, and all too plain for people to see. It can be painful for us, and uncomfortable for them. It is said that Sir Winston Churchill always hated the portrait which the Lords and Commons commissioned Graham Sutherland to paint of him to mark his eightieth birthday. Churchill believed it showed a man in decline, which almost certainly it did. In spite of all his great achievements, by that time Churchill was well past his prime, and had suffered a series of strokes, not helped by his own well-known eccentric lifestyle. It is said that after his death, Lady Churchill, who shared her husband's dislike of the portrait, had it burned.

Nevertheless, vulnerability is by no means altogether a negative quality, and in our third age, it can have positive benefits. A lady, to whom I had administered anointing and the laying-on of hands, wrote to me afterwards to express her gratitude. She said in her letter that I had healing hands, and urged me to continue to use this gift. This was the first time in my many years of ministry that anyone had ever said this to me. I was glad that the lady felt that she had benefited from receiving the sacrament, but I remained cautious about her words. I think it might have been truer to say that she sensed that my feeling of vulnerability matched hers. Although it was I who was administering the sacrament, it was not simply a case of my giving and her receiving. As I ministered to her, so she was ministering to me through her support and her prayers. So we shared our vulnerability, laid it before God, and both of us sought God's healing.

Those of us in later life can offer our vulnerability as a source of understanding, support, encouragement and healing to people of any age who, for whatever reason, may feel themselves to be vulnerable. We offer no ready answers or easy solutions, but our vulnerability can be a useful antidote to so much in our world, and, I feel, within our churches, which seeks to be powerful and triumphalist, aggressive and abrasive. We can only make sense of so many of the problems of life by believing that vulnerability lies at the heart of God. The theme is prefigured in the Old Testament where Isaiah speaks of the suffering servant as "a man of sorrows and acquainted with grief". The prophecy is fulfilled in Jesus, who "came not to be served but to serve, and to give his life a ransom for many". In the Garden of Gethsemane, on the night before he died, Jesus faced the ordeal which he knew lay ahead of him, and, with human vulnerability, he shrank from the prospect: "Father, if you are willing, remove this cup from me; yet not my will, but yours be done." Jesus recognised his vulnerability, and made it his offering to God.

As we recognise increasing vulnerability in later life, we can see it as a quality which comes from God, and which we share with God. It is part of God's life which we grow into and make our own.

> *Father, we remember the words*
> *of your apostle Paul,*
> *"whenever I am weak, then I am strong."*
> *We lay before you the vulnerability*
> *of our later years.*
> *Use it, we pray,*
> *in the service of your Church,*
> *to bring understanding and support,*
> *encouragement and healing,*
> *to those in need,*
> *to our divided Church,*
> *and to our troubled world,*
> *in the name of Jesus Christ, our Lord. Amen.*

Strain and stress

The day before my 74th birthday, I woke up and went downstairs to make an early-morning cup of tea. I made the tea, as I thought, and carried the tray back upstairs to the bedroom. It was only when I came to stir the pot, before I poured the tea, that I noticed that the brew looked thin and particularly watery. No wonder! I had omitted the most essential ingredient. In spite of the thousands of times I must have made the early-morning tea, this time I had forgotten the tea bag. So the last day of my seventy-third year started with some degree of strain and stress: strain, because reluctant knees had to make an extra journey up and down stairs in the early morning; stress, because of the realisation that I had failed to complete a minor daily routine. Even though I could laugh at myself and see the joke, the incident served to remind me that I was getting older. Tomorrow would bring another birthday to mark the inexorable passage of time.

Yet, I reflected as I sat in bed drinking my tea, my level of stress was probably as nothing compared with that of the people I saw passing our house on their way to work that morning. Apart from the stress of travelling on crowded trains and buses, they would be facing all kinds of stress when they got to work: decisions to be made, deadlines to be met, routines to observe. The human relationships surrounding them would make or mar their day. They would probably have to cope with an avalanche of words coming to them from many different directions, and the never-ending demands of constant communication.

It is not surprising, then, that one of the most popular hymns continues to be "Dear Lord and Father of mankind". Its popularity lies in the fact that it speaks to us all, at whatever stage of life. Yet it is not a new hymn, nor, in fact, was it ever intended to be one. The lines were written by John Greenleaf Whittier, an American poet of the nineteenth century, who, as a Quaker, was not accustomed to hymns as a part of Christian worship. He was writing at a time of much unrest and social strain and stress, comparable in its own way with what we experience now.

Strain and stress have always been with us and made their impact on people's lives. We see this at work in the Bible. The story of Elijah in the Old Testament tells how he has done battle with the false prophets of Israel, and put them to the sword. He is exhausted, and comes eventually to a cave on Mount Horeb. There God speaks to him, and Elijah recognises God in the "sound of sheer silence". It was this silence and awareness of God's presence that Jesus sought in order to bring him refreshment and renewal amid the strain and stress of his ministry. So after he fed the people with the five loaves and two fish, he made the disciples get into a boat and go on to the other side of the lake. He would follow later. "After he had dismissed the crowds, he went up the mountain by himself to pray." Strengthened by the silence of the place, and his communion with God, Jesus was ready to face more demands, further stress. In spite of the storm that had blown up, he came to the disciples walking on the water, and called upon Peter to do the same. Even though Peter's nerve failed, Jesus proved to be a safeguard, and "when they got into the boat, the wind ceased".

There must be many times when we wish the wind that buffets us with many strains and stresses in later life would cease. Realistically, the strains that we experience may not be all that great or life-threatening, but for those of us who experience it, the stress is real enough. I can afford to laugh at myself for forgetting to put the tea bag in the pot, but I am also aware that my energy level is not what it was. Things that I once took in my stride, I now notice take more time and effort. There are always concerns about money and the maintenance of the house. It takes more effort to sustain relationships with old friends who live at a distance, and if they become unwell, we wish that we were nearer so that we could do more to help. It seems less than satisfactory to have to restrict our contact to what we hope is a supportive telephone call, although, we tell ourselves, that is better than nothing.

So we pray in the words of John Whittier that God will take from our lives "the strain and stress". Perhaps this is too much to ask for, and more than we should expect, no matter how attractive the prospect appears. We do need at least some degree of strain and stress to keep us alive and active, to provide us with stimulus and purpose in life. I remember a wise and experienced ward sister who every so often would sit two querulous old ladies side by side in the day room. She knew an argument would be bound to ensue, but that the argument would be harmless, and would help to keep the two old ladies mentally alert. This was good, insightful pastoral care which the ward sister was exercising for the good of her patients, but it is very different from the "ordered lives" through which the hymn suggests we should know the "beauty of God 's peace".

I have always found it difficult to order my life, even in retirement – perhaps especially in retirement. But just as Jesus went up the hill to be alone and to be with God, having fed the crowd and sent them on their way, so somehow, somewhere, we need to be able to order our lives so that we can find space for God. Within that space, we find that we too are nourished, the negative translated into positive. Strain and stress may not be entirely removed, but they can at least be set against, perhaps even transformed into, thanksgiving – for our lives, the years we have lived and our experience of life, for the support of family and friends, and the relationships that have sustained and nurtured us across the years. So we may come to know within ourselves something of the "peace of God which surpasses all understanding". May it guard our "hearts and minds in Christ Jesus".

> *God of peace,*
> *we lay before you*
> *the strains and stresses*
> *which we experience in later life,*
> *the frustrations we feel*
> *in acknowledging the decline*
> *of physical strength and mental energy.*
> *Grant us to know*
> *that we share the needs of our Lord*
> *for places of rest, and moments of quiet*
> *to be aware of your presence,*
> *so that strain can become thanksgiving*
> *for what has gone before,*
> *and stress become our confidence*
> *in whatever lies ahead.*
> *We ask this in the name*
> *of the Prince of Peace. Amen.*

Pushing back the boundaries

I went to the local supermarket to do our weekly shopping. I was in good time, so parking was no problem. Nevertheless, there were cars without permits parked in areas reserved for families, and for people with problems of mobility. Like most supermarkets, the display stand of daily newspapers is situated just by the main entrance. To pick one up, I had to push past people who were just "browsing", reading papers they had no intention of buying. As it was a day during the school holidays, there were lots of children running up and down the shopping aisles as if they were in the school playground. One boy had his roller blades on, and a little girl was riding her scooter. And so on. It was just one of those days.

The point of describing the scenario in some detail is not to introduce a familiar third age complaint that things aren't what they used to be. What caught my attention that morning was how the limits of what is regarded as acceptable behaviour are being extended all the time. Boundaries are constantly being pushed back in every area of life. Marriage, for example, is no longer regarded as the prerequisite and foundation stone of the family, and cohabitation is an acceptable part of life. Same-sex relationships can now be registered as civil partnerships within the law.

UK trading laws have been revised such that Sunday has become a day much like any other. Shopping has become recognised as an important part of the leisure industry, and integrated into our accepted pattern of life.

But we are no exception. If we look at ourselves as an age group, those of us in later life are also pushing back the boundaries as never before. At least one supermarket chain has introduced a policy of actively recruiting older people because they are thought to be more reliable than their younger counterparts. Some people start up new business ventures when they retire from full-time employment. Others give generously of their time and personal commitment to the voluntary sector. I have read a report which suggested that the over-fifties now account for more than 80% of the wealth in the United Kingdom. Almost a quarter said they took frequent holidays, and felt under no obligation to leave money for their children to inherit. We probably all know of people who have achieved great things in later life. Perhaps we have been able to do that ourselves, and experience a feeling of real satisfaction. It is certainly all very different from what it was when my parents were about the same age as I am now.

I would like to think that the boundaries we push back are not only physical, social and economic, but spiritual as well. I believe that later life should give us the freedom to think, and read, and wonder about God in ways that we find stimulating and nourishing, and which meet our own deepest needs. Old habits die hard. We may feel guilty, or at least vaguely uncomfortable, in pushing back the boundaries and constraints of received belief and teaching. But we have no need to feel bad about doing this. Our faith is centred on Jesus who spent much of his ministry challenging attitudes and pushing back boundaries. The phrase "Woe to you, scribes and Pharisees" occurs no fewer than five times in Matthew 23. Jesus denounced those who were guardians of traditions which locked people into outworn practices and debilitated them to no useful purpose, rather than leading them to God. Jesus was pushing the boundaries, but, in earthly terms, they proved more powerful than he was. Entrenched attitudes closed in upon him, and ensured that he paid the price with his life.

Later life gives us our last opportunity to re-examine and redefine our personal and spiritual boundaries. We may need to push them back in order to accommodate the person we have grown into. As we do so, we shall find that we are pushing back our boundaries in the direction of God.

Father,
forgive us for the boundaries
which we set around ourselves,
boundaries of attitude and outlook,
of race and colour, of religion and faith.
In later life,
give us strength of mind
and courage of purpose,
to push back the boundaries
which keep us from you,
and to discover the fullness of your love
revealed to us in your Son,
Jesus Christ our Lord. Amen.

Clearing out the clutter

My mother was not exactly a hoarder, but, being a very cautious person, she experienced real difficulty in persuading herself that there were many things she did not need to keep. So, to be on the safe side, she kept cartons, jars, wrapping paper, pieces of string, all kinds of things, just in case they might come in useful at some stage. In spite of some good-natured teasing and persuasion from the family, she maintained her habit to the end of her life. It made her feel secure and comfortable, so in the end all we could do was go along with it. Whatever we thought, this was what she wanted, and the way she chose to operate.

There is a bit of this in all of us, and we can recognise it as such. However, there may come a point where the reluctance to throw things away becomes hoarding, and hoarding can reach a point where it takes over people's lives, and life becomes impossible. People find that they cannot cope with the amount of goods they have accumulated. Our elder daughter runs a business which helps people "de-clutter" their houses. One person she visited could hardly let her in the front door because of the accumulation of clutter. When she eventually got inside, there was nowhere to sit. Every available surface was piled high. So on one level, our daughter is working simply to help people de-clutter their homes. On another, she is showing them how to reclaim their lives, and encouraging them to make a fresh start. They can enjoy their new-found freedom, knowing that they have faced up to their problem, and gone some way in dealing with it. They have the satisfaction of seeing the clutter removed, and of being able to enjoy the resulting space. At a deeper level still, they are helped to confront the real underlying problem as to why they feel the need to accumulate things in this way. Perhaps it is a kind of comfort mechanism, like eating sweet things in time of stress. Perhaps it is a kind of compensation for feelings of loss following some traumatic incident in their lives. Perhaps it is a means of coping with depression. Once the clutter is removed, which is the immediate and presenting problem, the person is then free to confront, in their own way, whatever it is that is really troubling them.

We can recognise these types of clutter easily enough, both physical and emotional. What is less obvious, and perhaps more difficult to see or admit to, is the religious clutter which so easily surrounds and clings to those of us who profess our Christian faith. Church vestries are notorious for housing religious clutter. They bear witness to our reluctance to throw anything away that has a religious connection. In my time, I have spent hours de-cluttering vestries of old service sheets, palm crosses, stubs of old candles, notices of meetings, and posters advertising events that took place long since in the past. Even so, it has always been a conservative de-clutter, because I have a strong regard for history, and would not wish to discard anything that could be of use to historians in the future.

But religious clutter exists in other places, far beyond the dust and mustiness of vestries, and within the walls of our churches. It exists, far more significantly, within our minds, and affects our outlook on our faith. When I was a young parish priest, and wanting to try things out, the one remark I did not want to hear was "We've never done it that way before." As I grew older, and more experienced, I learned to reply that we would at least try it out, and if it was not a success, whatever it was I was trying to experiment with, we could go back to what had always been done before. What applies to parishes, churches, institutions in general, applies equally to each one of us. We need to de-clutter our faith. The religious baggage we carry weighs heavily upon us. We find ourselves stuck in entrenched positions, holding outlooks and opinions that are no longer relevant or applicable. We may find that we have too little space left for the things that really matter in our faith. Ultimately we may find that we have very little space for God.

The problem is not a new one for religious people. Jesus told the parable of the Good Samaritan to the lawyer who questioned him and sought a narrow, definable and legalistic answer to the question, "Who is my neighbour ?" The parable pointed out in the clearest possible terms that anyone in need is our neighbour, regardless of religion, race, or social class. "Do not be conformed to this world," wrote St Paul to the Church at Rome, encouraging its members to get rid of the clutter of culture, expectations and habits of their way of life before they became Christians. Instead he urged them to be "transformed" by the renewing of their minds, so that they could determine the will of God – "what is good and acceptable and perfect". In other words, make space for God in your hearts and in your lives.

In the book of Revelation, the New Testament ends with the vision of "A new heaven and a new earth". The "holy city, the new Jerusalem comes down out of heaven from God". The one who is seated on the throne says, "See, I am making all things new." All the clutter of life as we know it is removed, including death and mourning and crying and pain. God is all in all. All this is a vision for the future, but even in later life – perhaps even especially in later life – we need to keep before us some kind of vision towards which we can move, and by which we can measure our progress. We can look at our outer lives, and see what there is we can get rid of. It is always useful to have more space. What is essential is to look at our inner lives, to inspect them critically, even ruthlessly. When we have got rid of the clutter, we shall find that there is ample space for God.

Heavenly Father,
look mercifully upon us
when we fill our lives
with the abundance
of the things you have given us,
and leave no space for you.
Give us the courage
to look critically at our faith,
so that we may open ourselves to you,
and in the space we have created, come and dwell
  with us,
and show us the vision of your glory
in your Son, Jesus Christ our Lord. Amen.

Moving on

During my last three years as a hospital chaplain, I took part in the annual Christmas pantomime. Like so many other in-house shows, it provided an opportunity for the staff to let their hair down, display a wide variety of talents other than their professional skills, and generally get their own back on the institution that employed them, and, for better or worse, largely directed their way of life.

The year after I retired, I was asked to take part again as a replacement for a member of the cast who had dropped out at short notice. The next year, the producer was short of men, so again asked me to help out. I attended a couple of rehearsals, and then made my apologies. I had been made most welcome, there was no question of that, but I felt uncomfortable within myself. The comradeship and mutual understanding that were born of common concerns and shared experiences no longer existed and drew us together. I was conscious that our ways had inevitably diverged. I knew that they had moved on, and so had I.

Perhaps I had moved on farther than they had. As long as I have known it, the NHS has always been in a state of flux, with one reorganisation following hard on the heels of another. But at least those who were still members of staff were working in a familiar environment, no matter how much it was changing around them. In contrast, I had passed through, or perhaps was still passing through, one of the major changes in life and lifestyle, and finding the process far from easy. To be back in my old surroundings, and in contact with former colleagues with whom I had shared so much in the past, was a reminder of the feeling of loss that retirement had brought with it. It has something to do with the dignity and status that we feel daily work confers upon us, no matter how much we may complain about it at the time. Nevertheless, there was enough of me still in good working order, and with enough insight, to recognise that moving on was not only an inevitable, if painful, part of the process of retirement, but actually good in itself. I was aware that something was growing and rising out of the feeling of loss, though what shape it would grow into, and in what direction it would rise, I had no idea. That was something I found disconcerting rather than exciting. I am not a great one for exploring paths and roads that do not appear on maps.

In spite of my uncertainty, however, some things did become clear. For example, status no longer bothered me. I am what I am. I hope people will accept me as such. As for dignity, a couple of visits to the hospital out-patients' department for intimate examinations have relieved me of any unrealistic pretensions on that score, and I am prepared to trade my original hair colour for the benefits of senior citizens' travel discounts, and concessionary rates to all kinds of events and attractions.

It is tempting to put the process into biblical terms, and to say that I have moved on through the wilderness of giving up work, and into the promised land of retirement. Of course that would be an exaggeration, but I have discovered, no doubt like many others in later life, that one of the secrets – if not disciplines – is to keep moving on, in order to explore, and, all being well, to fulfil, at least some of the promises that life still has in store for us. When Jesus said, "I came that they may have life, and have it abundantly," he was offering those words to everyone without restriction, not to any one particular age group. I love the words of the prophecy of restoration in Isaiah 65: " I am about to create new heavens and a new earth... No more shall there be in it...an old person who does not live out a lifetime, for one who dies at a hundred years will be considered a youth..."

To "live out a lifetime" involves moving on, and maintains our essential youthful approach to life. There is still so much for us to discover, about God's creation, about God's new creation revealed in Jesus, and about the part God wants us to play within it. In later life, we move on to explore those truths as fully as we can.

Heavenly Father,
your Son, our Lord Jesus Christ,
moved on from place to place in his ministry
to proclaim your love,
and bring the Good News of your Kingdom to
    many.
Give us the courage, in later years,
to follow his example,
and by moving on,
to continue to explore
his promise of life in all its fullness
to those who believe in him,
now, and in the world to come. Amen.

Travelling light

Our house has two major storage areas. Both are in the space between the roof and the bedroom ceilings, and are not easily accessible. It is at least three years since I put anything into one area, and probably longer than that since I took anything out of the other. I know we have a lot of things stored up there, but, with a few exceptions, I have forgotten what. I shall not find out unless I investigate again. So I have to ask myself why am I keeping it all. If I do not know, or have forgotten what is stored, and if I have not seen it, needed it, used it or missed it for all this time, why don't I just get rid of the whole lot ? That would be the simplest and most obvious thing to do.

Unfortunately, what appears to be a straightforward question fails to elicit an equally direct answer. Although I cannot now remember exactly what is stored, I do know that many of the things are there because we find them difficult to throw away. They have, as we say, sentimental value. In other words, they carry with them something of our personal history, and that makes me reluctant to discard them. I know that we store our memories in our mind, and most of us carry a rich store with us that we are only too ready and willing to talk about in our third age. Nevertheless, tangible souvenirs do evoke memories and past feelings within us that otherwise become buried beneath the passage of time. On that score, we hesitate to part with them, and feel a sense of loss if we do.

On the other hand, there is a voice within that tells us we should be travelling light in our third age. Not only should we be gradually reducing our collection of material possessions, we should also find it helpful to offload some of the emotional and spiritual accretions that we have either accumulated, or that have attached themselves to us over the years.

As part of travelling light, we may need to let go of old scores, forgive old hurts, remove the burden of blame from other people, and the guilt with which we so easily load ourselves. We may also need to give up entrenched attitudes and fixed positions, especially in our religious faith and outlook. All the great world religions suffer from this, and Christianity is no exception. Yet much of Jesus' teaching was directed against the entrenched attitudes of the religious traditions and practices of his own time. He denounced the scribes and Pharisees as "Blind guides! You strain out a gnat, but swallow a camel." And his parable contrasted the attitudes of the Pharisee and the tax-collector. The one thanked God for his righteousness according to the Jewish law, and that he was "not like other people". The other "would not even look up to heaven," but prayed "God be merciful to me, a sinner!" The self-righteous and well-established Pharisee stands in stark contrast to the penitence of the tax-collector, an outcast of society. The message for us is as clear as when Jesus first told the parable. We need to get rid of entrenched positions that make life in general, and religious faith in particular, difficult if not impossible, both for ourselves, and for other people.

It is sad to see buildings, ideas, traditions, which formed part of the fabric of our lives, torn down, discarded, or considered to be no longer relevant or of any use. That is part of the burden of later life. Yet it is also a reminder of how much we invest in the external things of life, and how much we look to them for the comfortable support of familiarity. We can feel bereft, and experience a real sense of loss, at least temporarily, when they are no longer there. Perhaps there is within us something of Peter on the mount of Transfiguration. It was such a wonderful experience that he wanted to cling on to it, prolong it. So he suggested making three shelters, one each for Jesus, Moses and Elijah. In doing so, he missed the point entirely, and the meaning of the moment passed him by. It is something that we learn in later life, perhaps in ways that can be quite costly for us. In order to approach God, and to be with God, we need to travel light.

> *"What can be seen is temporary,*
> *but what cannot be seen is eternal."*
> *Father, we give thanks*
> *for these words of your apostle Paul.*
> *May they encourage us*
> *to shed all that weighs upon us,*
> *encumbers us and hinders us,*
> *so that we may travel light*
> *on the journey that leads us to you. Amen.*

Use it or lose it

All of us in our third age are familiar with senior moments, those instants of forgetfulness when we lose our train of thought or have a complete blank as to what it was we were going to do next. "What are you looking for?" asks my wife. "A brain," I reply. "If you find one, it's mine!" It's a standing joke, and long may it remain no more than that. Perhaps we know people suffering mental problems due to age, and the thought lurks at the back of our minds that it could happen to us as well. Alzheimer's is not a new or uncommon phenomenon, but the illness of Iris Murdoch, the books written about her by her husband, Professor John Bayley, and the film made of her life, have brought the disease to the forefront of public consciousness, and especially to the attention of those of us in our third age. One article I read about Alzheimer's suggested that its onset could be delayed, if not prevented, by an active lifestyle, both physically and mentally. For all of us in our third age, the message is "use it – or lose it".

Each one of us will make our own choice as to what we will do. One of the fascinating things about the third age is the vast range of interests to pursue, and the number of organisations with which we can become involved. One of the key texts for me in the New Testament is 1 Corinthians 12:4, "There are varieties of gifts, but the same Spirit." I offered myself for the ordained ministry because I felt that God was calling me to use the gifts he had given me in this particular way. As I approached retirement and tried to think what lay ahead, I realised that although I had used many of my gifts during my ministry, I had by no means used them all. There were others which had necessarily been put to one side over the years, and which were now waiting for me to rediscover and explore at my leisure. This has probably been true for many of us throughout life. The third age brings with it the opportunity to expand our horizons, maybe in all kinds of unlikely and unexpected directions. This is stimulating, fulfilling, and wholly good.

So I find myself volunteering to undertake a number of commitments which make a combination of physical and mental demands on me. I derive much satisfaction from knowing that I am still fit and active enough to meet the situation and handle it competently. The adrenalin still flows, and I am profoundly thankful that it does. I have been presented with a challenge, and I have been able to meet it successfully. In fairness, I have to admit to one or two occasions when I have not been up to the mark. I have to acknowledge that I am not as young or as adaptable as I was, and not take on things that are now beyond me.

However, our activity can be directed inwardly as well as outwardly. For example, I have gathered up the many photographs that I have taken over the years and assembled them in an ordered collection. My purpose is to create memories, in so far as it is possible consciously to do this. As I look at my photographs again, I can recall the situations and circumstances in which I took them, and the events which they record. If there comes a time when I am less active and unable to be involved in things as I am now, I will have created my own source of reminiscence therapy.

Another direction which I am pursuing inwardly is my own spirituality. I am trying to look at the whole question of what God is doing among us, and in us, and through us in our third age, and in particular, within me. So I try to reflect on what God is saying to me in later life. Is it different from any other stage of life, simply because of the passage of time, or is it essentially the same? If God's call in earlier years was to service and activity, to what is God calling me now, when I am less active than I was? Do I have a different understanding of God in my third age? Is there such a thing as a spirituality of the third age? If so, is it recognisable? How can it be recognised? And, most importantly, is it generally recognised by the Church? Above all, where is the Spirit leading those of us in later life, and how?

All these are questions which I ask myself. Sometimes I wish I didn't, and I wish they would go away, because the answers are unclear and uncertain, if they exist at all. They leave me feeling unsettled and uncomfortable, at a time of life when I wish I could organise my faith as easily as I do my photographs. But in my heart of hearts, I recognise that that is not possible. I know only too well, that if I don't continue to use and develop my spirituality, I shall, like any other part of life, eventually and inevitably lose it. I often recall a blessing pronounced by Donald Coggan at the end of a service I attended when he was Archbishop of York: "The disturbance of the Holy Spirit be with you always." As I look back, I realise that that disturbance has always been there, and still is. It keeps me alive both outwardly, and inwardly towards God. Perhaps it is God's way of encouraging me to go on exploring and deepening my understanding of the faith. "Use it," I hear him saying. "Don't lose it or let it go."

Lord God, Holy Spirit,
we give thanks
for the variety of gifts
you have given to each one of us;
for those that we have knowingly
used in your service,
and for those
that remain to be explored
in later life.
Give us the vision
to see them, and know them, and use them,
so that nothing may be lost,
but our lives deepened and enriched
by the ever-growing understanding
of the love made known to us
in Jesus Christ our Lord. Amen.

I am still learning

I went to buy a present for an old friend who was celebrating the twenty-fifth anniversary of his ordination to the priesthood – his silver jubilee. I went to a religious bookshop not really knowing what I should choose. My choice did not take long. There, hanging up behind the counter, was a plaque in bronze carrying the simple inscription, "I am still learning." This was a quotation from Michelangelo, still learning despite his eighty-seven years.

I thought these words would be an encouragement to my friend, who likes to read and study and to go on learning, but in retrospect, I think they would be more appropriate hanging on the wall over my own desk. They are a reminder that our minds must remain active and involved, those "little grey cells", as Hercule Poirot often calls them. It is interesting that Agatha Christie's two great detectives are both of mature years: Poirot, though travelling about, always seems to be in the right place at the right time to solve the crime and, as it usually is, bring the murderer to justice. Miss Marple, on the other hand, seems to sit and knit and think things through until she makes the vital connection between them. Then, with their true significance revealed, she is able to point to the guilty person.

There are many different ways we can choose to keep our little grey cells working, even though in later years we lose millions every day. I remember, for example, a study day led by Bishop Tom Butler for his clergy in the Anglican diocese of Southwark. He used his own mathematical background to deliver two addresses about God, first "God Pure", then "God Applied". I am no mathematician, and I could not reproduce what he was saying without reference to his written text. No matter. The important thing was that I could recognise even as he was speaking that the bishop was leading me into new territory. He was introducing me to new concepts, new ways of thinking about God. Even though I could not fully understand them, I was aware that I was being opened up to new ideas. In a way, it was uncomfortable and disturbing. My well-established and, as far as I am aware, my reasonably well-worked-out ideas about God were being subjected to scrutiny. Here was someone who, with the best possible intentions, was threatening to dig up my tramlines. I might even end up by finding myself rerouted, travelling an unknown track and in a different direction. Heaven forbid! But at the same time, I found the experience refreshing and stimulating, enough to prove to myself that I was still alive, both mentally and spiritually. It gave me a great boost to know that, as Michelangelo said, I am still learning, and wanting to learn, about God.

Learning about God can be a neglected area for keeping our grey cells alive and in good working order. Arguably, our form of worship is too often a passive experience. We sit in well-ordered rows, presumably listening and paying respectful attention to what the people at the front are saying and doing. I have often wished, when I have been preaching, that someone would have the courage to stand up and challenge what I was saying. Now that I sit in the pew more often, I wish that I had the courage myself to voice a contrary point of view. As it is, good manners prevail. I sit and fidget, or just "switch off" altogether and think my own thoughts. But I am always sad when I find myself doing this. We so much need to go on stretching our minds and keeping our grey cells alive and active, and what better way of doing this than by deepening our understanding of so many different aspects of our Christian faith. It can be stimulating, exciting, and yes, even fun. We may well find that we want to come back for more.

In the Gospels we see Jesus involved in discussions with people who wanted to ask him questions about their religious faith. We note, however, that they did not always receive the answers they wanted or expected. The man who asked Jesus what he should do to inherit eternal life was told to sell all that he owned and distribute his money to the poor, then come and follow Jesus. "But when the man heard this, he became sad for he was very rich." As we explore our faith in later life, we may not receive the answers that we expect, or feel we need, or hope for. Perhaps that is of lesser importance. What matters is that we are still learning: learning about ourselves, and learning about God.

Heavenly Father,
we give you thanks
for all your gifts,
especially those of thought and learning,
of perception and understanding.
In our later years,
help us to keep our minds alive
by exploring new aspects of life,
and by visiting again
the wide compass of our Christian faith,
exploring afresh its meaning,
the depths of its wisdom and understanding.
There may we find
new life and new love
in the infinite riches of your being
made known to us in your Son,
Jesus Christ our Lord. Amen.

What a wonderful world

Louis Armstrong was arguably the most popular of all the great jazz musicians. He was an outstanding trumpet player, and made many recordings from the early days of the gramophone in the 1920s until his death in 1971. But on what is possibly his best-known record, he is not playing his trumpet, but singing in his own distinct, gravelly voice. The song is called "What a wonderful world".

The words are sentimental, even trite, but no more so than Mrs Alexander's "All things bright and beautiful," a hymn of enduring popularity. I find them running through my mind on many occasions and in many different places: the enveloping silence of the North Yorkshire moors; the brilliant light of a summer's day on the Suffolk coast; the spectacular sunsets over Morecambe Bay in mid summer, and those over London in late autumn. When I was Chaplain of Guy's Hospital, I witnessed at first hand the skilful art of the practice of medicine. I am constantly astounded by the ever-increasing discoveries of science and technology. I truly wish I had the skill and craftsmanship of people who work with their hands, and can see how to turn ideas into objects which are ingenious and beautiful in themselves. All these speak to me not only of a wonderful world, but of God's wonderful world.

It is a world of which God approved: "God saw everything that he had made, and indeed, it was very good." Even so, creation could not work by itself. It needed to be shaped, organised and directed. So the second creation story in Genesis tells of the man and the woman being formed and placed in the Garden of Eden to order it on God's behalf. It was a high calling, as the psalmist expressed: "When I look at your heavens ... the moon and the stars which you have established; what are human beings that you care for them? Yet you have made them a little lower than God ... You have given them dominion over the works of your hands." We are called to be pro-creators, in every sense of the word, on behalf of God in creation, but we have failed to live up to our calling. The story of Adam and Eve is of universal application. It tells of how we have all betrayed God's trust.

Since I retired, I have tried to catch up on the appreciation and understanding of art and literature and classical music which, for various reasons, passed me by in my younger days. As I have read books, listened to music, and contemplated great paintings, I have become aware that they, too, represent, and are part of, God's wonderful world. How tragic it is that humankind, which can produce and appreciate such beauty, can also ravage it and destroy it in equal measure. War and violence assail us on every side. The natural environment faces destruction. Plants and animals are threatened with extinction.

I discovered that even the spectacular sunsets over London in the late autumn are the result of pollution in the atmosphere. As in the story of Adam and Eve, we are confronted by the paradox of human nature: we are capable of scaling sublime heights, expressing the best that is in the human soul. Conversely, we are capable of descending to the depths of indescribable degradation, both of ourselves and of others.

It was this paradox of the human condition that Jesus took upon himself when he was born into our world. The prologue to St John's Gospel expresses this for us: "He came to what was his own, and his own people did not accept him. But to all who received him, who believed in his name, he gave power to become children of God." John was writing in the light and knowledge of the resurrection as the basis of our belief. Although he does not mention it explicitly, the "power" to which he refers is power of the resurrection of Jesus. So the paradox is complete. Jesus takes our worst, and makes of it his best. Even the Eden Project in Cornwall was created out of the industrial scars of old china-clay workings. God takes our mess, and makes out of it something to which the human can relate, and to which it can aspire.

Every day, amongst all the bad news that is heaped upon us, there are countless acts of human kindness which are not thought worthy of mention. Self-giving is taken for granted, and usually goes unreported. This is the pattern of God's involvement in our life. God takes our death and gives us resurrection, And when I see this, and ponder this truth as I grow older, I say to myself, "What a wonderful world."

> *Father, Creator,*
> *we give thanks to you*
> *for your wonderful world,*
> *that Jesus, your Son,*
> *was born among us,*
> *and brought us the gift*
> *of eternal life,*
> *Amen.*